Alberto Ramon, [illegible] *th the I Ching*, teaches us how to have the Universe speak to us when we have questions through the tools of the *I Ching*. Alberto, through his insight on how to look at the information from the *I Ching*, has made the *I Ching* a relevant tool for intuitive decision making for the 21st century individual.

Jerry Gin, Ph.D., Chairman,
Foundation for Mind-Being Research

Alberto Ramon is utterly devoted to the science and art of the *I Ching*. His book provides important innovations in its use that make its ancient wisdom much more accessible and understandable to the non-specialist.

Byron Belitsos, coauthor of
The Adventure of Being Human

Conversations with the I Ching is a fascinating new perspective on the ancient *I Ching*. Taking his background in engineering, Alberto has used his rigorous left brain as a solid base for a right brain, meditative, and intuitive leap to a new vision and understanding of this valuable life resource.

Bobbie Heyman, M.A., Coordinator,
Institute of Noetic Sciences Community,
Diablo Chapter

Conversations with the I Ching is a superb teaching tool. It guides the student of the *I Ching* with many readings and clear explanations. I recommend it to anyone who wants to use the power of the *I Ching* to facilitate the decision making and creative processes.

Garrett Riegg, attorney and metaphysical teacher

Alberto's unique approach to *I Ching* interpretation gives us a new tool for personal empowerment.

Karen Jackson, founder of Gratitude Power - Center for Heart Inspired Living

Alberto explains the Hexagrams so wisely that the *I Ching* is much more accessible to everyone. I love the simplicity. This book is a guide that is easy to follow to the otherwise obscure readings of the *I Ching*, a key that opens the gate to self-discovery at the intuitive level and gives self-nourishment for the peace of mind and soul.

Dr. Sonia Gaemi/Hashemi, author of *Eating Wisely for Hormonal Balance* and Chair of Women for Cultural Wisdom, Co-Chair of the Committee for Women's Human Rights of the United Nations Association of San Francisco.

In *Conversations with the I Ching*, Alberto Ramon seems to apply Systems Theory, an interdisciplinary approach to investigate the principles common to complex entities, to facilitate the use of this ancient wisdom tool, the *I Ching*. As an engineer with a bent for Eastern wisdom and Western metaphysics, he is the logical choice to achieve this alignment.

Bett Lujan Martinez, M.Ed.,
Executive Director, The Possible Society of California

Alberto Ramon's book, *Conversations with the I Ching*, shows a new way of obtaining life's meaningful answers, interpreted via the *I Ching*. See for yourself how this book can empower you and the lives of others.

Dr. Christopher Colgin, D.C.,
Bay Area Laser Center

Conversations with the I Ching

An Intuitive Approach to Understanding the Answers

With 85 Explained Readings

ALBERTO RAMON

Conversations with the I Ching
An Intuitive Approach to Understanding the Answers

ISBN: 9781721678082

Printed in the United States of America

Cover design by Lund Arts, john@lundarts.net

Clarity and simplicity. Those were my motivations for writing this book. I believe that's how Spirit speaks through the I Ching. Many influences assisted me, all pointing in the same direction. The first influence was from Carl G. Jung.

A wise man's question contains half the answer.

— Solomon Ibn Gabirol

This book is dedicated to Deborah Pierce and Patty Casentini for their invaluable contribution in making it more clear.

I would also like to acknowledge:

Claudette Gregg for her thorough editing,
John Lund for his magnificent cover design,
Rafael Campo, Ila Maki, and Alexandra de Avalon
for their revisions and helpful suggestions,
Shanti Haydon for her support and help
in making this book more attractive,
Graciela Chichilnisky for her constant
support and encouragement,
Norma Fox for her excellent design
of TheLogicOfChance.com

Introduction: Make the Symbols Speak

The *I Ching* is one of the oldest books in history. It originated in China over 3,000 years ago, and today is being used all over the world to access one's intuition and gain insight. It contains sixty-four symbols called Hexagrams (from the Greek for "pictures"), which can metaphorically describe any situation or course of action.

Each Hexagram is a figure composed of six stacked horizontal *lines,* with each *line* either a Yang (male; unbroken; —) or Yin (female; broken; - -). Each Hexagram has a name and sections (the *Judgment;* the *Image*; the *Lines,* and their respective commentaries), which explain what the Hexagram is about.

The person asking a question (referred to as the inquirer) tosses three coins of equal value six times, which produces one or two Hexagrams, depending on results to be discussed later. These results, once interpreted, always give an insightful answer, even if the inquirer is unfamiliar with the *I Ching.*

All questions and castings appear to trigger an intelligent force that overcomes chance by pointing to the answer. This is true even if the *I Ching* appears not to answer a question, because that in itself is an implicitly negative answer. Since this intelligent force influences the castings of the coins, perhaps it can also influence other kinds of events.

A complete interpretation of the result from a reading should be a clear message, rather than a collection of texts. One good analogy would be a jigsaw puzzle: after all the pieces have been put together in a certain way, an image emerges. The individual pieces are still seen, but only as part of the image.

The purpose of this book is to show you how to translate the result from a reading into a clear message in plain language, so there can be a conversation between you and the *I Ching*. For this purpose, new attributes such as the *applicable meanings* of a Hexagram and the *theme* of a reading will be introduced in Chapter II.

II. Every Reading Has a Theme

The set of 64 Hexagrams viewed as whole symbols has the potential to express in a reading anything that can be significant. For this reason, each Hexagram has multiple meanings, as explained in the next section. For example, Hexagram 59, Dispersion, could also mean, as a whole symbol, sharing, distributing, marketing, etc. However, for any given reading, only a few of the meanings of the resulting Hexagram or Hexagrams relate to the question asked, the surrounding situation, or the main issue. These are the *applicable meanings* to the reading.

When I interpret an *I Ching* reading, I first determine the *applicable meanings* of the resulting Hexagram or Hexagrams. If necessary, I use the Dictionary of the 64 Hexagrams, which appears at the end of this book, for all the possible meanings of the Hexagram or Hexagrams.

Then I recognize the most significant phrase formed by all the *applicable meanings* combined. I call it the *theme* of the reading. In my experience, the *theme* is the starting point for interpreting a response because it describes the big picture of the response, the frame of reference. It's an overall message providing essential information that guides the interpretation. The *theme* may answer the posed question, refer to the surrounding situation, or refer to the main issue. It always means something relevant.

Then I consider the resulting texts from the Hexagrams, especially any moving *Lines*, as clues to be interpreted in relation to the *theme*. They may enrich the *theme* with more information, give an answer if the *theme* does not, or point to the correct *theme* or *themes* if some of the significant phrases are conflicting. Positive moving *Lines* tend to reinforce the *answer* while negative moving *Lines* could be warnings that restrict or qualify the *answer*.

It is very important not to assume that the *theme* always answers the posed question. This is a common interpretation error. Both the *theme* and the resulting texts, combined, always convey a significant message and the answer may be given by a text. See the readings in Chapters VII, VIII, and IX for all cases.

If the answer can't be found anywhere, it is implicitly negative, and a new possibility is usually suggested, because the *I Ching* always points to progress.

I use the Wilhelm/Baynes version of the *I Ching* for the names of the Hexagrams, their texts, and their respective commentaries.

III. A Brief Explanation of the Intuitive Approach to Understanding the Answers and How it Originated

In the past, intuition was never my strength. I always felt that it was beyond my comprehension. Raised as the son of a psychiatrist and professor of neurology at the University of Buenos Aires, I grew up in an environment in which the development of the intellect was considered the most important activity, to be pursued through study, especially academic work. My idea of wisdom was a combination of knowledge, clear reasoning, and moral values.

The scientific method was the model to be used for the acquisition of any kind of knowledge. Intuition might perhaps play a part, but only after hard work and the exhaustive use of the other faculties. My father, quoting Thomas Edison, was fond of saying, "Genius is ninety percent perspiration and ten percent inspiration."

Believing that decision-making is a purely logical process, I was frequently paralyzed by indecision when I did not feel that I had enough information to make "rational" choices. I often opted for what seemed to be the most "reasonable" alternative, not always with the best results.

During my college years, I had a hard time making decisions about my future career. Several possibilities appeared to be equally appropriate, and there were no clear-cut facts to help me to choose one course of action over another.

I recall thumbing through a copy of the *I Ching*, the ancient Chinese book of divination, at a bookstore and quickly dismissing it. A month later, I overcame my initial skepticism when I learned that the world-renowned psychiatrist Carl Jung had used it extensively to contact his intuition. The mere thought that I could use my intui-tion to make wise life decisions gave me the confidence that I needed to complete my academic studies. I decided that, after graduating, I would investigate this system with an open mind and no preconceptions.

When I started consulting the *I Ching*, I was amazed by the clarity and relevance of some results, which made me feel that I was communicating with an enlightened being. Other results, however, seemed obscure and unrelated to my questions. For this reason, I misunderstood many readings. Frustrated by my inability to make sense of those readings, one day I seriously considered ending my involvement with the *I Ching*.

But that night, a revelation suddenly came to me in a dream. "Look at the big picture," it said. "It provides a basis for understanding all the clues. That's the way intuition works and the way to awaken it."

That advice urged me to perceive situations and *I Ching* responses *holistically*. The resulting texts from a reading (which are the *Judgments*, the *Images*, and any moving *Lines*) are to be considered as clues to be interpreted in relation to a big picture. I realized that I had been interpreting readings in a fragmentary manner because I had been reading those texts without any reference to a big picture. It is easy to make the mistake, as I did, of focusing on the appealing parts of a reading without understanding it as a whole, thereby misinterpreting it.

A Brief Explanation of the Intuitive Approach

I researched every available book on the *I Ching*, hoping to find guidance about how to determine the big picture as a basis for interpreting a reading, or at least to see if the authors offered any other interpretive approaches. All I could find were intricate explanations of the structure of the Hexagrams and sometimes interpreted readings without any explanation of how the author arrived at the interpretation.

Since I couldn't find any interpretive methods, I was inspired to create a step-by-step approach based on the advice that I had received in my dream. As it turned out, this approach revealed a structure of the *I Ching* symbolic language and an inner logic underlying the result of a reading, so the result could be understood as a clear answer in plain language.

Obviously, "look at the big picture" implies "start interpreting readings with the resulting Hexagrams to be understood intuitively as whole symbols, not as a collection of texts." Viewed in this way, the sixty-four Hexagrams have the potential to express in a reading any possible big picture, which means anything that can be significant to the reader.

Here is what I believe is the simplest and most logical structure of the *I Ching* for that to be possible: The set of sixty-four Hexagrams represents a comprehensive spectrum of concepts about situations, actions, events, etc., that can be significant in a reading. Each Hexagram represents a distinct category of this spectrum—which is the range of the Hexagram's meanings. However, for any given reading, only a few meanings of the resulting Hexagram or Hexagrams will be *applicable.*[1]

With that structure in mind, I studied each Hexagram as a whole symbol in the Wilhelm/Baynes book and other translations of the *I Ching* to discover which concepts make that Hexagram unique.

For every Hexagram, I observed which possible situations, actions, events, etc., could be represented *only* by that Hexagram. I also expanded some concepts to equivalent concepts in other contexts. For example, I extended "campaign" in Hexagram 7, The Army, to "project." I made sure that all the concepts that I assigned to a Hexagram are compatible, and that none of those concepts is better suited to another Hexagram. That is how I built the range of possible meanings of each Hexagram. This range of meanings must be the same for everyone who obtains that Hexagram in a reading, but the *applicable meanings* will depend on each situation.

Realizing that the *I Ching* is a comprehensive and timeless divination system, I expanded the list of meanings of each Hexagram to include modern situations. Then I started interpreting readings using holistic perception, according to my dream, and the Dictionary of the 64 Hexagrams.

Then, for every reading, I observed the phrases formed by the *applicable meanings* of the resulting Hexagram or Hexagrams until I recognized the most significant phrase, which I called the *theme*.

---

[1]The *applicable meanings* of a Hexagram are those that relate to the question asked, the surrounding situation, or the main issue.

A Brief Explanation of the Intuitive Approach

For a reading resulting in two Hexagrams, I combined the *applicable meanings* of the first Hexagram with the *applicable meanings* of the second to show the possible *themes*. Those meanings were connected according to *patterns* that were easy to recognize, such as "cause–effect," "initial situation–future situation," "prerequisite–desired result," and a few more. One of these combinations made sense for that reading, revealing the *theme*. That's how *pattern recognition* helped my intuition to recognize the *theme*. With practice, this process became almost immediate, because it's similar to the process for understanding sentences in common language. (For a description of all the *patterns* I have observed, see the "Symbolic Syntax" chapter.)

I noticed that the *theme* often pointed to the answer. If not, it described the surrounding situation or the main issue, but it was always relevant. In this case, the texts—any moving *Lines*, the *Images* and *Judgments*—sometimes revealed the answer. If no answer could be found, it was implicitly negative.

Classifying my readings according to this simple rule greatly facilitated their interpretation. Since the *I Ching* always points to progress, when the answer was negative, it usually revealed a new perspective. In this case, I did a second reading, with a question that was more pointed or from another angle, to confirm the new perspective. This technique, called cross-checking a reading with a new one, is a form of critical thinking. I also used this technique to confirm any interpretations I made that I was unsure of, whether the answer was positive or negative.

Sometimes any moving *Line* in the upper half of a Hexagram (the upper trigram) could be about a future action or situation beyond the *theme*, or a warning.

In those readings where the *theme* pointed to the answer, the texts enriched the *theme* with more information. However, if a reading had several possible *themes* revealing incompatible messages, the texts pointed to the correct *theme* or *themes*. If necessary, the interpretation of a reading took into account the interpretation of recent readings about the same subject.

I reviewed past unclear readings, done by myself and by others, using the approach I just described, with the benefit of hindsight, and suddenly the *theme* and the texts made sense, revealing a clear and complete answer.

In the final analysis, I realized that the result of a reading has been completely interpreted if my intuition synthesized all its parts into a meaningful whole, which could be larger than the answer that I sought. That was *the message of the reading*.

In some instances, if I wanted more information from a reading, to make an interpretation more precise, or to confirm a prior interpretation, I did further readings with related and even opposite questions. In other words, I had a full conversation with the *I Ching* so all my doubts were cleared. The reader is encouraged to do the same.

IV. A Vehicle to Your Intuition

Life is complex and full of challenges. We can't expect to make important decisions as if they were problems in an algebra class. There are usually too many unknowns. Or the amount of data is just unmanageable. The logical approach works only when we have complete and adequate information at hand. That's not the case in a complicated and unpredictable world, especially when human beings are involved.

According to the great American psychic Edgar Cayce, "The more and more each is impelled by that which is intuitive…, the greater, the farther, the deeper, the broader, the more constructive may be the result."

For thousands of years, the *I Ching* has been used in China and other countries as a tool for accessing one's intuition by asking questions. The *I Ching* always gives the answer, whether the question is simple or profound, general or specific, so long as it is legitimate.

Advice from the *I Ching* can imply a prediction, for it takes into account unexpected events that might occur after the consultation, so the answer is always timely. Thus, the *I Ching* can enable you to make sense of your circumstances and take charge of your life.

The *I Ching* is future-oriented. It is a practical tool for personal growth because when you ask appropriate questions, it can: (a) suggest actions that bring about self-fulfillment; (b) put events in perspective; and (c) clarify your feelings. It can also be an ideal addition to journal writing because it can enrich your thoughts and experiences with deeply intuitive answers.

Conversations with the I Ching

The *I Ching* is also a tool for inspiration, creativity, and problem-solving. It can enable you to think "outside the box" and generate your best ideas. Moreover, a creative state of mind tends to inspire even more powerful questions to the *I Ching*.

The *I Ching* can also be used to predict the final outcome of an ongoing situation, such as the result of a recent job interview. In general, any future situation that will eventually be known by you and does *not* depend on your future actions can be predicted by the *I Ching* now.

For example, the *I Ching* can be consulted to predict the results of an election. However, if the future situation depends on future actions that you may take, the *I Ching* will only give you advice on what to do to obtain the most fulfilling result. Although this book presents all types of readings, most of the readings discussed here are for advice, not for prediction.

The fact that intuition and precognition exist implies that the human mind can access a level of reality that is beyond space and time. In the case of the *I Ching*, anyone who does a reading may be triggering an intelligent force that influences the coins, and possibly the surrounding environment, to convey meaningful information.

Perhaps someday Quantum Physics will explain this fact as an extension of the Observer Effect, the fact that the act of observing a particle affects its behavior, which reveals the role of one's higher consciousness in the physical world.

V. A Key Question Will Unleash Your Creativity

There are two ways for your intuition to get an answer to a question: either wait for a dream, an insight, or a synchronicity; or instead, take an active role and consult an oracle like the *I Ching*. The active approach, while it gets immediate answers, requires key questions in order to get clear answers.

According to Albert Einstein, "To raise new questions, new possibilities, to regard old problems from a new angle, requires creative imagination and marks real advances." In other words, the quality of your questions determines the quality of the answers. Create strategic and empowering questions about new possibilities, avoiding preconceptions and any attachment to an outcome.

The key question depends on the existing situation, as discussed below. Formulating a key question facilitates the interpretation of a reading, because that question, by addressing the real issue, could get a clear and direct response, which may be easy to interpret. Be aware that the *I Ching* sometimes does not just answer your question, but a larger or more appropriate question.

If you are not sure what to ask the *I Ching*, take time to clear your mind so that you can see the big picture and recognize the main issue.[2] Then you can phrase the question in the simplest terms and be open to any possible answer.

---

[2]Two effective ways to achieve this purpose are meditation and *HeartMath.* The latter is a technique for creating coherence between the brain and the heart.

Conversations with the I Ching

Every personal reading applies only to the individual seeking the answer at the time of the consultation. An appropriate question must have no ambiguity and preferably address only one issue.

Readings with open-ended questions, which typically start with "what," "how," "why," or "which," are the most likely to elicit explicit answers.

Readings with yes/no questions are preferable for deciding or predicting between two possibilities and also can be used for confirming the interpretation of a previous reading.

Should you arrive at more than one question, choose the one that puts you in charge of all your possibilities. For example, **"How do I decide about this applicant?"** (advice is more empowering than **"What will be the result of hiring this applicant?"** (prediction, because this applicant may not be the best alternative, so why try to predict it? Most of the readings in this book are for advice.

Questions about the future of an *ongoing* personal situation or relationship will get a meaningful answer. However, "fortune telling" questions about a hypothetical personal event in the future may only get advice. Frivolous or selfish questions may receive only a corrective answer. As a rule, anything that you'll eventually become aware of or experience, whether personal or public, you can predict *now*.

The following are some possible cases:

If the issue under consideration is simple, like whether to accept a job offer or to predict the result of an interview, the question could be: "How shall I decide about this job offer?" or "What will be the result of the interview?"

A Key Question will Unleash your Creativity

A complex and uncertain situation can be approached with this simple question: "What do I need to know about this situation?" The answer typically will explain the situation and give advice on how to proceed.

If the existing situation is known but a new direction is needed to move forward, a good question is: "Given this situation, what is the best course of action?"

Suppose the question is open-ended and there are several possible choices, like "What strategy should I use?" or "What career should I choose?" Because the *I Ching* deals with qualities, find an attribute by which the choices are *conceptually distinct* before doing a reading, so the result of the reading would point to only one choice, or perhaps to a new choice.

If the response from the *I Ching* is incomprehensible, even after cross-checking the reading with a new one, probably the question was too specific, which excluded some possible answers. Or the question was inappropriate by assuming a situation that may not happen.

The following example illustrates an implicitly negative answer and the importance of asking a key question to avoid an incorrect interpretation. Steven met Helen at a party, chatted with her briefly, and managed to get her phone number. Before calling her, he wanted to know what to expect. So he asked the *I Ching*, "What is the existing situation between Helen and me?"

He obtained Hexagram 61, "Inner Truth," which is about depth, intimacy, and authenticity, and Hexagram 27, "Providing Nourishment," which is about nourishing and cultivating. So the *theme* was: "If the conversation is sincere and deep, cultivate a friendship." Steven found this surprising because he knew that he had not established a deep connection with Helen.

Nevertheless, due to his wishful thinking, he felt encouraged by this result to call Helen and leave a message on her voicemail. However, she never called him back. Then he painfully realized that he had gotten an answer that contradicted his experience. This disconnection is how the *I Ching* says, "Nothing is going on." A key question would have been: "What happened between Helen and me at the party?"

Avoid over-analyzing. Most problems have an underlying pattern that can be identified in a few readings. Excessive questioning may result in unrelated results.

Finally, the *I Ching* should not be approached as a "machine" for answering questions. It should be viewed instead as a vehicle to communicate with your higher consciousness, your living source of inspiration and intuition.

Some key questions

How do I go about creating ...?
How is ... to be accomplished?
Given this situation, what is the best course of action?
Given this situation, what should be my decision?
Given this situation, what do I need to know to make the best decision?
How should I decide about this applicant?
What action must I take to transform this situation? How does this problem/challenge create a new opportunity?
What career should I choose? (complex inquiry)
This case is discussed on page 19.

A Key Question will Unleash your Creativity

At this stage of my project, what should I be focusing on now?
If I do ..., what will be the result?
What is the state of ... and how will it evolve?
Why do I get this advice?
Should I give up on ...? This is a good confirmatory question.
How should I decide between A and B? (either/or question) Typically, the answer will point to A or B, provided that there are clear differences between them.

Questions that should be avoided
Is it OK to go ahead with the project and have John as an associate? These are two separate issues. Questions should address preferably one issue. It is better to use an open-ended question.
Will I find a romantic relationship this year? This is a fortune telling question. The *I Ching* will give you advice on what you can do to improve your chances, not a blind prediction. There will be simply too many factors involved and too many decisions you'll make every day to being able to make any prediction. A more appropriate question is: *How can I improve my chances of finding a romantic relationship?*
Will such and such position be suitable for me? The position has not yet been offered. This question is assuming a situation that may not occur. It is better to ask: *Should I apply to such and such position?*
When will this event occur? The *I Ching* does not give dates. It is preferable to ask *Will this event occur between this and that date?*

Will my son/daughter visit me this year? This is a question about another person. A more appropriate question could be: Will I be seeing my son/daughter sometime this year? *Please tell me about this person* or *What kind of year will this one be for me?* These questions are too vague. *What is the best time to buy gold?* The *I Ching* does not give dates or perform calculations. A more appropriate question could be: *How will I benefit if I buy gold now?* The answer may depend on how long the buyer intends to keep it.

VI. Symbolic Syntax

Pattern recognition facilitates the interpretation of every reading that consists of two Hexagrams. There is at least one pattern by which the *applicable meanings* of both Hexagrams are meaningfully connected forming the *theme* of that reading. Symbolic Syntax is the set of all patterns that form a *theme* for the readings that I observed.

For the sake of simplicity, let *A* be the *applicable meaning* of the first Hexagram and *B* be the *applicable meaning* of the second Hexagram for a given reading. Each represents what is significant in the reading, whether a personal action or a situation, personal or public.

1. *Initial Situation–Future Situation:* Given the initial situation *A* (present or past, *B* is a future situation. If *B* is a desired outcome, the answer is advice for achieving *B* by following the suggestions in the texts. If *B* is an undesired outcome, the answer is a warning to avoid or minimize *B* by following the suggestions in the texts.

2. *Prerequisite–Desired Result: A* is a prerequisite to obtain outcome *B*. If *B* is desirable, then *A* already tells you what to do. If *B* is undesirable, the answer is a warning to avoid or minimize *B* by doing *A*. If *A* is not true or doable, the answer is negative.

3. *Cause–Effect/Manifestation: A* causes *B*, where *A* is a required action, and *B* is the desired outcome. If *B* denotes an undesired outcome, the answer is a warning to avoid or minimize *B* by doing *A*. *(Example of a Positive Answer: The more you exercise, the healthier you will be.*

Example of a Negative Answer: The more you drink alcohol, the less healthy you will be.

4. *Advice Pattern:* Given *A* (the present situation, *B* should be done. In some cases, *B* modifies *A*; in other cases, it does not. *(Examples: With modification of A: Since your car is dead, you should charge the battery. Without modification of A: Since you're here, we should have a talk.)*

5. *Choice Pattern:* The one asking the question must choose either *A* or *B*. *(Example: Either you go with your family or you don't go at all.)*

6. *Combination Pattern*: The one asking the question must choose both *A* and *B*. *(Example: You should be clear, and you should persevere.)*

NOTE: Patterns 1 through 4 are the ones I have observed most frequently. These patterns can be best understood by reviewing some readings included in this book.

The Case of a Reading Resulting in one Hexagram.

If a casting yields only one Hexagram, all the *applicable meanings* of the Hexagram, appropriately combined to make sense, form the *theme* of the reading.

VII. Readings That Give a Strong Answer

In the following readings, the answer is mainly given by the *theme*—that is, the most significant phrase formed with the *applicable* Hexagram *meanings*. Strong answers can be positive or negative, but negative strong answers are rare.

If there is any contradiction between the *theme* and any of the texts, the *theme* takes precedence, and the contradicting text can be regarded as a precautionary warning, a temporary situation, or a future event or possibility.

In some cases, as we will see below, the texts can help the reader to recognize the correct *theme* when two or more significant phrases give conflicting messages.

Conversations with the I Ching

How should I publish my book?

I wasn't sure whether to self-publish this book or to find a traditional publisher. So, I asked the *I Ching,* "How should I publish my book?" and I obtained Hexagram 41, "Decrease." By consulting the Dictionary of the 64 Hexagrams, I found that the concept of expenses was most relevant to my question. That concept can relate to money, energy, or time.

My casting included two moving *Lines*, the first and the fifth, which produced Hexagram 59, "Dispersion." When I consulted the Dictionary of 64 Hexagrams, I found a list of 53 concepts under Hexagram 59 that might relate to my question. By going over the list intuitively very quickly, I selected *spreading* and *distributing* as the concepts most relevant to my question.

Combining these Hexagrams resulted in two *themes*: (a) "The cost should be spread among the various activities" and (b) "After spending money, you will need to distribute the book." Both *themes* are not about associating with a publishing company, but about the cost of several services by other people (editing, printing, distributing, marketing, etc.) and also about doing some distributing myself. Since working with a traditional publisher would not require me to pay any money, this result was about self-publishing.

Line 1 in Hexagram 41 says, "Going quickly when one's tasks are finished is without blame, but one must reflect on how much one may decrease others." This means that achieving my goal more easily with self-publishing should not be at the expense of another goal, such as the quality of the book.

Line 5 says, “Someone does indeed increase him. Ten pairs of tortoises cannot oppose it. Supreme good fortune.” This implies that I would benefit by using someone’s services or reading a book on self-publishing.

The *Image* in Hexagram 59 says, “The kings of old sacrificed to the Lord and built temples,” which again refers to spending money to create something valuable. So, I self-published the book.

Why do I choose men who are emotionally unavailable?

This was a question posed by Sarah, who had a recurring pattern of getting romantically involved with emotionally unavailable men. She obtained Hexagram 24, “Return,” recurring, reaction, recovery, renewal, going back.[3]

There are three significant *themes* here. *Recurring* refers to similar situations she had been in, in the past. *Reaction* and *Going back* indicate that she was reacting to what had happened to her in the past, perhaps involving her father. *Recovery* is about healing from her present condition.

The *Judgment* says, “Return. Success. Going out and coming in without error. Friends come without blame. To and fro goes the way. On the seventh day comes return. It furthers one to have somewhere to go.” This implied that Sarah’s recovery could be successful. She needed to express her feelings (“going out”) and introspect (“coming

---

[3]In the following readings, the words after the Hexagram names are their *applicable meanings* from the Dictionary of 64 Hexagrams.

in". *Friends* could also refer to people who can support her, including therapists. The recovery may take time, which is indicated by *seventh day*.

The *Image* says, "The kings of antiquity closed the passes at the time of solstice. Merchants and strangers did not go about, and the ruler did not travel through the provinces." This may suggest that Sarah should not get romantically involved for the time being until her recovery from her last romantic relationship is complete.

How should I see this relationship that didn't work out?

After having a heated argument with her boyfriend, Peter, Mary decided to end the relationship. Later on, she consulted the *I Ching* about the meaning of the relationship she had just ended. When she asked her question, she obtained Hexagram 6, "Conflict," dispute, and Hexagram 32, "Duration," long-lasting, ongoing, persisting.

Putting both Hexagrams together, the following phrases can be formed: "*From conflict to enduring relationship*," "*(Despite) conflict, persist (in the relationship)*," and "*Conflicts will be ongoing.*"

Line 3 says, "To nourish oneself on ancient virtue induces perseverance. Danger. In the end, good fortune comes. If by chance you are in the service of a king, seek not works." This *Line* counsels discretion and not being too forceful.

Line 5 says, "To contend before him brings supreme good fortune." In other words, get advice from someone who can see both sides of the dispute.

Line 6 says, "Even if by chance a leather belt is bestowed on one, by the end of a morning it will have been snatched away three times." This means that pursuing the conflict to the end will not work. *Lines* 3 and 5 imply a positive outlook, whereas *Line* 6 is a warning in case Mary does not follow the advice given by *Lines* 3 and 5.

There is no advice anywhere in this result for Mary to contact Peter to save the relationship. However, the next day, Mary received a call from Peter, during which they worked out all their problems.

How do we choose the place of birth for our child?

Ralph lived in Florida with his wife, Marta, who was pregnant and expected to give birth in about four months. They were concerned that if there were any problem during the delivery, they would incur big expenses, given the high hospitalization costs in the United States and their inadequate medical insurance.

One alternative would have been for them to go to Marta's native country, Venezuela, for the childbirth, since hospitalization there was more affordable, and the services were very good.

However, this would have required a lengthy and inconvenient trip, considering Ralph's work commitments. So he asked the above question.

The result was Hexagram 42, "Increase," beneficial, generosity, and Hexagram 30, "The Clinging, Fire," light, guide, clarity. By combining both Hexagrams, the following *theme* can be formed: "*The generous services provided will be your guide.*"

Line 3 says, "One is enriched through unfortunate events. No blame, if you are sincere and walk in the middle, and report with a seal to the prince." This implies that even something unfortunate such as the need to travel abroad will work to the couple's advantage.

Line 4 says, "If you walk in the middle and report to the prince, he will follow. It furthers one to be used in the removal of the capital." This refers to someone trustworthy for a difficult task—in this case, a doctor.

Line 5 says, "If in truth you have a kind heart, ask not. Supreme good fortune. Truly, kindness will be recognized as your virtue." This points to good and free or inexpensive services due to socialized medicine in Venezuela.

Based on this reading, Ralph and Marta went to Venezuela for the birth of their son, which was successful and affordable.

Why am I losing clients?

Tamara owned a very successful gym. However, she had recently been losing clients. So, she asked, "Why am I losing clients?" She obtained Hexagram 49, "Revolution," change, and Hexagram 55, "Abundance," many.

The combination of both Hexagrams yields the following *theme*: "*By changing to another gym, people get more services than you are offering."*

Tamara learned that in fact there were many other gyms that were offering services like hers, and for the same price or less.

Line 4 in Hexagram 49 says, "Changing the form of government brings good fortune." This refers to the need to reorganize and innovate to stay ahead of the competition.

The *Image* of Hexagram 55 says, "Thus the superior man decides lawsuits and carries out punishments." So, Tamara successfully sued the competitors who were illegally offering her proprietary products or using similar business names.

What should I do about my pain?

Dora experienced unbearable pain in her right knee and in her lower back due to osteoarthritis. She asked, "What should I do about my pain?" The result consisted of Hexagram 26, "The Taming Power of the Great," taming, restraining and Hexagram 14, "Possession in Great Measure," position, placed. These meanings form the following *theme*: "*Constrict your knee so it will be in the right position.*"

Line 4 says, "The headboard of a young bull. Great good fortune." This means that before a bull's horns grow out, a headboard is fastened to its forehead, so that later when the horns appear they cannot do harm. A good way to restrain wild force is to forestall it. This is about taking preventive action to avoid future problems. So, Dora used a knee band, which kept her knee in place and alleviated her pain.

Is this relationship going to evolve into a serious one?

Marilyn felt disappointed about her relationship with John. They had been involved for two years, and now he was getting ready to go to Europe for three months for business reasons, without ever having talked about getting engaged. So, Marilyn asked, "Is this relationship going to evolve into a serious one?" She obtained Hexagram 61, "Inner Truth," authentic, sincere, serious, and Hexagram 27, "Providing Nourishment," cultivating, providing. The combination of these two Hexagrams forms the *theme*: "*If the relationship is real and authentic, cultivate it.*"

Line 2 says, "I have a good goblet. I will share it with you." *Line* 5 says, "He possesses truth, which links together." Both *Line*s refer to sincerity and trustworthiness.

To make sure that John's intentions were serious, Marilyn had a talk with him in which she brought up her doubts. He expressed deep sorrow about having to leave her and offered financial support in case she had any need or decided to travel to Europe to visit him. Marilyn felt reassured. Later on, John bought her a roundtrip ticket to London. Eventually, they got married.

What does the I Ching have to say about Carl Jung's intention to write a foreword to the English edition?

In the foreword to the English edition of *The I Ching or Book of Changes* by Wilhelm and Baynes, Carl Jung describes how he submitted two questions to the *I Ching*. The first one is quoted above. He obtained Hexagram 50, "The Cauldron," instrument of transformation, which he interpreted as the *I Ching* itself, and Hexagram 35, "Progress," gain, advancement. Therefore, the *theme* is: "*The I Ching will gain status as a result of Jung's action.*"

Line 2 says, "There is food in the ting [cauldron]. My comrades are envious, but they cannot harm me. Good fortune." This suggested that the new translation would compete successfully with the existing ones.

Line 3 says, "The handle of the ting is altered. One is impeded in his way of life. Once rain falls, remorse is spent. Good fortune comes in the end." This suggested that there could be difficulties in interpreting readings even with this edition, but there would always be an understanding, once mental blocks were cleared.

What comment does the *I Ching* have about Carl Jung's writing the foreword?

After he started to write the foreword to the *I Ching*, Jung asked it to comment on his action. The result consisted of Hexagram 29, "The Abysmal," risk, abyss, infinite, the unknown, the subconscious, and Hexagram 48, "The Well," source, useful, available.

The combination of both symbols forms this *theme*: "*Taking a risk so the unknown and the subconscious can become available to people as a source of knowledge through the I Ching.*" This refers to Jung risking his reputation by tackling a subject that has no validity among the scientific establishment.

Line 3 says, "Forward and backward, abyss on abyss. In danger like this, pause at first and wait, otherwise you will fall into a pit in the abyss. Do not act this way." In the context of the *theme*, this *Line* counsels prudence in using the *I Ching* and patience in studying its answers to avoid making incorrect interpretations.

The *Image* in Hexagram 29 says, "The superior man walks in lasting virtue and carries on the business of teaching." This refers to the importance of the foreword's explanation of the *I Ching*.

The *Image* in Hexagram 48 says, "Thus the superior man encourages people at their work and exhorts them to help one another." This could mean that the *I Ching* is an inspiring and problem-solving tool. Jung felt reassured. (NOTE: This and the previous reading are reinterpretations of Jung's readings.)

What should I do about my slow computer?

My computer became too slow after running for more than an hour. When I asked this question, I got Hexagram 18, "Work on What Has Been Spoiled," decay, disrepair, and Hexagram 26, "The Taming Power of the Great," holding back, inhibiting. The *theme* is: *"There is decay; something needs to be inhibited."* Since my antivirus program was constantly running, I disabled it. That corrected the problem.

Line 1 says, "Setting right what has been spoiled by the father." According to the commentary in the Wilhelm/Baynes book, *father* stands for the past. This was advice to fix something that had been neglected, such as replacing the antivirus program. That solved the problem.

Readings That Give a Strong Answer

How can I avoid overreacting when I feel frustrated?

Marian had a tendency to react abruptly and sometimes sarcastically when she had any disagreements with her boyfriend, especially when she was stressed out.

Concerned about the effects that her behavior was having on the relationship, she wanted to find a way to control herself, so she asked the above question. She obtained Hexagram 5, "Waiting," patience, waiting for the right occasion, and Hexagram 43,"Break-through," resoluteness, making known, outburst. The *theme* of this reading is: *"Be patient and wait for the right occasion to make things known, to avoid an outburst."*

Line 4 says, "Waiting in blood. Get out of the pit." The comment of this *Line* in the Wilhelm/Baynes book says that composure is the only way of getting out of a dangerous situation. The *Image* in Hexagram 43 says, "Thus the superior man dispenses riches downward and refrains from resting on his virtue," advising kindness and openness.

Predicting the outcome of a war

In *I Ching—The Book of Change*, English author and scholar John Blofeld describes how he consulted the *I Ching* to predict the outcome of the war between China and India in 1962. His reading indicated that the invasion would end very quickly and without much territorial gain. When he did the reading, China had already invaded Indian land over an old border dispute.

He obtained Hexagram 48, "The Well," utilizing, taking advantage, available, and Hexagram 63, "After Completion," conclusion, ending. Combining both Hexagrams produces this *theme*: "*China took advantage of the situation and will end the operation.*"

Line 1 says, "One does not drink the mud of the well. No animals come to an old well." In the context of the *theme*, this could mean that not much land would be taken.

Line 2 says, "At the well hole one shoots fishes. The jug is broken and leaks." If the jug is interpreted as support or maintenance, this could mean that it would have been hard for China to maintain any additional captured territory or that there would have been no international support for any further gains. By using the Hexagrams obtained by Mr. Blofeld, this reinterpretation reaches the same conclusion.

What careers should I be considering?

This question was posed by Angie, a 16-year-old high school student. She obtained Hexagram 56, "The Wanderer," briefly, exploring, trying things out, and Hexagram 55, "Abundance," many opportunities.

The *theme* of the reading is: "*The more possibilities you explore, the more opportunities you will have to find the right career.*"

Line 1 says, "If the wanderer busies himself with trivial things, he draws down misfortune upon himself." This warns against wasting time on trivial matters.

Line 6 says, "The wanderer laughs at first, then must needs lament and weep. Through carelessness he loses his cow. Misfortune." This warns against carelessness or taking things lightly.

The *Image* in Hexagram 55 says, "The superior man decides lawsuits and carries out punishments." This comment is about making decisions and carrying them out.

The *Image* in Hexagram 56 says, "The superior man is clear-minded and cautious in imposing penalties, and protracts no lawsuits." This advice is about being diligent and avoiding procrastination. Angie decided to explore different types of work.

Is coffee good for me?

Bob asked this question because he really enjoyed coffee, but was not sure if it was good for him. He obtained Hexagram 10, "Treading," conduct, proceeding cautiously one step at a time, and Hexagram 47, "Exhaustion," fatigue, frustration, irritability. By putting these Hexagrams together, the *theme* is: *"Proceed cautiously to avoid fatigue and irritability,"* which is a mildly affirmative statement with a warning.

Line 1 says, "Simple conduct. Progress without blame." This implies that a little amount of coffee is fine.

Line 6 says, "Look to your conduct and weigh the favorable signs. When everything is fulfilled, supreme good fortune comes." This could be advice to watch the effects of drinking coffee to make sure they are positive.

The *Image* in Hexagram 10 says, "Thus the superior man discriminates between high and low and thereby fortifies the thinking of the people." This is a suggestion to exercise good Judgment to receive the benefits of coffee and avoid its bad effects. (NOTE: This reading applies only to the person who asked the question.)

One result answers two questions

Rebecca and Bob were planning to finish remodeling their house in Pinole, California, before selling it, finding a new property in a nearby town, Benicia, and moving there. They had two questions. One of them was: *"How will living in Benicia work out for us?"* The other was: *"Is it preferable to get our house ready for sale first and then find a new place to live?"* The result was Hexagram 64, "Before Completion," almost, not totally, and Hexagram 44, "Coming to Meet," meeting needs, finding.

Line 3 says, "Before completion, attack brings misfortune. It furthers one to cross the great water." According to the Wilhelm/Baynes book, this implies that a new situation must be created before attempting to complete the transition.

Line 5 says, "Perseverance brings good fortune. No remorse. The light of the superior man is true. Good fortune." This indicates an eventual favorable situation. Hence, the *theme* formed with the Hexagram meanings is: *"Although Benicia does not have everything you want, it will meet your needs."*

However, since Hexagram 44 also stands for finding, another *theme* is: *"Before completing the remodeling, find a new property."* This could be the necessary new situation indicated by *Line* 3. This theme answers the second question. The next question, below, was about the type of property.

Readings That Give a Strong Answer

Should we buy a new house or just the land?

Rebecca and Bob were not sure whether to buy a new house or just the land upon which they could build a house to their liking. So they asked, *"Considering all the pros and cons, is it preferable to buy a new house or just the land?"* The result was Hexagram 31, "Influence," fascination, requesting.

In other words, the *theme* of the reading is, *"If you are fascinated by a property, make an offer."* The Judgment says: "To take a maiden to wife brings good fortune," which suggests a purchase. The *theme* is not about the type of property. The foremost consideration here is how Rebecca and Bob will feel about it.

Eventually, they found a beautiful piece of undeveloped land in Benicia, with panoramic views and lots of underground water. They felt so attracted to it that they stopped looking, made a bid, and bought the property.

They started to build a house and other facilities on it while still living in their current house and completing its remodeling.

How can I make my company more successful?

This reading and the next are reinterpretations of two readings from the book *"I Ching Readings—Interpreting the Answers,"* by Wu Wei. The following readings basically concur with the conclusions in that book.

Barry, the new president of a large equipment manufacturing company, was going to address the board of directors for the first time. Personal computers were becoming very important in the business world, so he believed that the company should immediately expand into computer manufacturing, or else risk being left behind and eventually driven out of business.

Barry needed to convince the board of directors, so he did a reading, asking the above question. He obtained Hexagram 64, "Before Completion," almost, not quite, and Hexagram 50 "The Cauldron," transforming, trans-muting, processing, tool. Certainly, the result was not about staying the course. The *theme* for the reading is: *"Given that the company is not quite up to its full poten-tial, it needs to be transformed."*

Line 3 says, "Before completion, attack brings misfortune. It furthers one to cross the great water." According to the Wilhelm/Baynes book, this implies that although the transformation would have a favorable outcome, a new situation had to be created first.

The key was in the *Image* of Hexagram 50: "Thus the superior man consolidates his fate by making his position correct." In other words, Barry needed to strengthen his position in the company before making any move. Unsure what the next step should be, he asked the next question.

What can I expect if I tell the Board of Directors that they should accept my recommendation to get into the computer business or else I will resign?

The result was Hexagram 63, "After Completion," completely, absolutely, everything, thorough, eventually, and Hexagram 49, "Revolution," change, replacement.

These are the *themes: "Either everything I want, or else they'll have to replace me"* and *"If I give a thorough presentation, they will eventually change their disposition."* This is a strongly positive result because the first *theme* confirms the question and the second gives the answer.

Line 4 says, "The finest clothes turn to rags. Be careful all day long." The *Image* in Hexagram 63 says, "Thus the superior man takes thought of misfortune and arms himself against it in advance." Both texts warn against the danger that the company could fall behind if it was not keeping up with the times.

The *Judgment* of Hexagram 49 says, significantly, "On your own day you are believed. Supreme success, furthering through perseverance. Remorse disappears."

So Barry gave a thorough presentation to the board with an ultimatum: either the board would have to accept his proposal or they will have to find another president. Despite the initial reluctance of the board, Barry eventually won their endorsement and was able to implement his ideas.

Am I prepared to take this exam?

Maurice had been studying very hard to take the prelim exam at the School of Engineering in order to enroll in the graduate program. He wanted to make sure he was well prepared, so he asked the above question. He obtained Hexagram 2, "The Receptive," undergoing, being subject to, and Hexagram 45, "Gathering Together," incorporating, joining.

The *theme* here is: "*You will be subject to an exam before you can join the graduate program.*" The *Image* of Hexagram 45 says, "Thus the superior man renews his weapons in order to meet the unforeseen." This refers to preparing well in order to deal with unexpected questions.

There are two *moving Lines* in Hexagram 2. *Line* 4 says, "A tied up sack. No blame, no praise." This counsels seclusion in order to concentrate on the preparation for the exam. *Line* 5 says, "A yellow lower garment brings supreme good fortune." According to the Wilhelm/Baynes book, this means discretion, that is, prudence in answering the questions to avoid taking too much time on any one, due to time constraints. Maurice passed the exam with high grades.

How should I resolve this conflict with the homeowners association?

Without being aware of the restrictions and regulations of his condominium complex, Jack installed a wooden enclosure in his backyard to protect his cats against the weather and to keep them locked in at night so they wouldn't be at risk by roaming around at that time. This enclosure was attached to his unit and was quite visible from other units.

Due to complaints from other homeowners the association demanded the removal of the enclosure. It had been over five years since the enclosure was installed so Jack considered rejecting the demand based on the California Statute of Limitations and also to keep his cats protected.

So he asked the *I Ching* the above question. The result consisted of Hexagram 33, "Retreat," backing off, moving away, and Hexagram 25, "Innocence (blameless). Therefore, the *theme* is: *"Move it away so you won't be at fault."*

Line 1 says, "At the tail in retreat. This is dangerous. One must not wish to undertake anything." In other words, do not be late in taking action because you may be penalized.

Line 3 says, "A halted retreat is nerve-wracking and dangerous. To retain people as men- and maidservants brings good fortune." This *Line* refers to retention. In other words, there was no need for a complete removal.

The *Image* of Hexagram 25 says, "Thus the kings of old, rich in virtue, and in harmony with the time, fostered and nourished all beings." This refers to the cats still being sheltered. Jack moved the enclosure away from the house and reduced its size, so it would not be very visible from other units. He also explained to the board of directors why he needed the enclosure. Eventually, he obtained the approval from the board.

How serious is my condition due to the high level of cholesterol?

Concerned about my very high level of cholesterol, I went to see a doctor. He strongly advised me to take cholesterol-reducing and blood-thinning medications, but I refused to do so because I was opposed to taking drugs.

Instead, I chose a gradual approach involving Niacin and more exercise. After all, I thought, being a vegetarian, my condition could not be that bad. However, I posed the above question out of curiosity. I obtained

Hexagram 31,"Influence," which stands for urging, prompting and Hexagram 39, "Obstruction," closed-minded, blockage.

The *themes* formed with these Hexagrams are: *"You were urged to take medications but were close-minded"* and *"If you are influenced to take action by his advice, you will avoid a blockage."*

Line 4 says, "If a man is agitated in mind, and his thoughts go hither and thither, only those friends on whom he fixes his conscious thoughts will follow." This could have referred to a high level of work-related stress that could have aggravated my condition and also to how my beliefs were limiting my possibilities.

The *Image* of Hexagram 31 says, "The superior man encourages people to approach him by his readiness to receive them." This counsels open-mindedness and could also refer to the doctor who saw me. The *Image* in Hexagram 39 says, "Thus the superior man turns his attention to himself and molds his character." This warned me to pay more attention to my condition.

However, I did not take this answer seriously and stayed with my gradual approach. Nine months later I had a heart attack due to blocked arteries and realized that I underestimated the seriousness of my condition.

Can I expect to have knee surgery by next year?

Tammy had a painful knee injury due to a car accident. She was concerned that the doctor she was seeing at the hospital had not prescribed knee surgery yet. So she asked the above question.

She obtained Hexagram 20, "Contemplation (View)," examining, considering surgery, and Hexagram 53, "Gradual Development," process, evolution. Both Hexagrams form this *theme*: *"You are being examined. The condition of your knee will be evolving (favorably)."*

Line 3 says, "Contemplation of my life decides the choice between advance and retreat." This refers to a decision that the doctor had to make about the surgery. The *Image* in Hexagram 53 says, "Thus the superior man abides in dignity and virtue, in order to improve the mores." All this says that things cannot be rushed but must proceed at their own pace for a maximum benefit to the patient.

The *Image* in Hexagram 20 says, "Thus the kings of old visited the regions of the world, contemplated the people and gave them instruction." This could refer to the doctor informing Tammy about her condition.

The *Judgment* in Hexagram 20 says, "The ablution has been made, but not yet the offering. Full of trust they look up to him," suggesting that although the surgery was not performed yet, she could trust the doctor. The knee surgery was performed six months later.

Can I expect to have my knee back to normal?

This was the second question Tammy asked. She obtained Hexagram 7, "The Army," campaign, regimen. This may refer to a long-term regimen involving physical therapy.

The *Image* says, "Thus the superior man increases his masses by generosity toward the people." This could refer to the benefits derived from the therapy.

Tammy was prescribed physical therapy for 19 weeks. The answer was not about "recovery" or "healing" but indirectly implies improvement. (Note: Since the answer is indirect, this reading actually belongs in Chapter VII but was placed here for continuity with the previous reading.)

How do I find an appropriate editor for my manuscript?

In response to this question, I obtained Hexagram 56, "The Wanderer," glimpse, trying out, exploring, and Hexagram 62, "Preponderance of the Small," exceeding, surpassing. The *theme* is: *"Try the editors on a short piece of work and one will surpass the rest."*

Line 6 says, "The bird's nest burns up. The wanderer laughs at first, then must needs lament and weep. Through carelessness he loses his cow. Misfortune." This is a warning against being careless in reviewing an editor's work and choosing the wrong editor.

The *Image* of Hexagram 62 says, "Thus in his conduct the superior man gives preponderance to reverence. In bereavement he gives preponderance to grief. In his expenditures he gives preponderance to thrift." This suggests paying attention to details in order to get the best possible work. It could also be advice to take the cost of editing into account.

Readings That Give a Strong Answer

What kind of description should I write on the back cover of my book?

I needed ideas for writing an attractive description, so I asked the above question. I obtained Hexagram 25, "Innocence (The Unexpected)," being unaware, having no idea, without preconceived notions and Hexagram 20, "Contemplation," considering. So the *theme* is: *"Those who have no idea about the I Ching will contemplate it. Consider them."*

The *Image* of Hexagram 20 says, "Thus the kings of old visited the regions of the world, contemplated the people, and gave them instruction." This could refer to doing presentations explaining and promoting my book. The *Image* of Hexagram 25 says, "Thus the kings of old, rich in virtue, and in harmony with the time, fostered and nourished all beings."

In other words, the description should address all kinds of people. As a result, the description and the book are written for those who know nothing about the *I Ching*, while presenting an innovative approach for those who are knowledgeable.

What would be the best model for Health Care in the U.S.?

The result consisted of Hexagram 42, "Increase," assisting, enhancing and Hexagram 36, "Darkening of the Light," injury, harm. The *theme* is: *"Assistance to keep people out of harm (suffering or financial ruin)."* *Line* 3 says, "One is enriched through unfortunate events. No blame, if you are sincere and walk in the middle, and report with a seal to the prince."

In other words, "*there should be assistance for people in unfortunate circumstances. They should be reported to someone with the authority to take care of them.*"

Line 5 says, "If in truth you have a kind heart, ask not. Supreme good fortune." This could mean that *"Patients should not abuse the system with unnecessary requests for services"* and *"Providers and insurers should not charge excessive rates."*

Line 6 says, "He brings increase to no one. Indeed, someone even strikes him." This could mean that *"Those who do not provide good service or charge unfair rates should be penalized."*

The *Image* of Hexagram 42 says, "Thus the superior man: if he sees good, he imitates it; if he has faults, he rids himself of them." This means that what works in other health care systems should be copied and what does not work should be discarded.

Will Britain vote to leave the European Union in 2016?

This reading was done June 15, 2016. The vote took place June 23. The result consisted of Hexagram 24, "Return," reversal, return to a previous situation and Hexagram 27, "The Corners of the Mouth," voicing, expressing. The *theme* is not about staying the course. So it is "*A reversal was voiced.*"

Line 6 says: "Missing the return. Misfortune. If armies are set marching in this way, one will in the end suffer a great defeat," indicating negative consequences.

As it turned out, the separatists prevailed and the British economy was adversely affected by the vote. The actual separation did not take place immediately because the formal request to secede was made months later.

What will be the result of the U.S. Presidential Election on November 8, 2016?

This reading was done November 3, 2016, with the polls showing Hillary Clinton beating Donald Trump. The result consisted of Hexagram 22, "Grace," attractive, charismatic, superficial and Hexagram 6, "Conflict," contentious, controversial, divisive. The *theme* of this reading is clearly about Trump.

After conducting a divisive campaign, Trump unexpectedly won the election but Clinton won the popular vote by 2.9 million votes. The Trump administration was plagued by numerous conflicts. Eventually Trump was impeached twice by the House of Representatives but was acquitted both times by the Republican-controlled Senate.

Another *theme* is that "*a superficial perception of issues fueled antagonistic views*." That could explain the outcome of this election.

What will be the outcome of the Coronavirus pandemic?

This reading was done in March 22, 2020. The result consisted of Hexagram 55, Abundance, magnitude and Hexagram 54, The Marrying Maiden, marriage, contract, duty. By combining the *applicable meanings* the *theme* is: "*Given the magnitude of this pandemic, everyone has a duty.*"

The *Image* of Hexagram 54 explains the duty: "Understanding the transitory in the light of the eternity of the end," which means understanding the sacrifices to be made so this epidemic can eventually be brought under control.

Lines 2 and 3 are about darkness due to the obstruction of the sun, which stands for clarity, so they stand for not knowing what to do. *Line* 2 is about rousing people through truth and education and *Line* 3 is about breaking one's arm, casualties.

The *Image* of Hexagram 55 is about making tough decisions. Since no positive outcome is mentioned, the implication is that it will take a long time for this to be achieved.

What's the most likely outcome of the 2020 U.S. Presidential Election on November 3?

This reading was done August 9, 2020. The result consisted of Hexagram 53, Gradual Progress and Hexagram 39, Obstruction. By combining those meanings, the *theme* of the reading is: *"Someone's gradual progress will be obstructed."*

Readings That Give a Strong Answer

However, *Line* 6 says: "The wild goose gradually draws near the cloud heights. Good fortune." This *Line*, being in the upper trigram, indicates a future event, the eventual completion of the ongoing process, winning the election.

The *Judgment* of Hexagram 53 says: "The maiden is given in marriage. Good fortune." This is about the presidential inauguration. The *Judgment* of Hexagram 39 says: "It furthers one to see the great man." This could indicate a higher authority confirming the result of the election, like Congress or the Supreme Court.

This response shows the rise of Joe Biden as a candidate, his electoral triumph, the obstruction and unsuccessful court challenges by the sitting president, Donald Trump, and Biden's inauguration January 20.

VIII. Readings That Give a Weak Answer

In the following readings, the *theme of the reading*[4] points to the surrounding situation or the main issue, and the answer is mainly in a resulting text—a *moving Line* in the first Hexagram if there are two Hexagrams, or the *Image* or *Judgment* in the Hexagram(s) obtained in the reading. For this type of reading, the answer is indirect and frequently positive. It could be conditional, optional, in the future, etc. Readings of this type, in which the answer is negative, are in Chapter IX, "Readings Giving a Negative Answer." A positive answer is not necessarily favorable but normally is.

[4] The *most significant phrase* formed with the *applicable meanings* of the resulting Hexagram(s).

Should I hire a professional editor to improve the quality of my manuscript?

I had worked very hard polishing the manuscript of this book, but still suspected that a professional editor could make it more clear and attractive. The result to this question was Hexagram 8, "Holding Together," in agreement, together, jointly, which implies working with someone else.

The *Image* says, "Thus the kings of antiquity bestowed the different states as fiefs[5] and cultivated friendly relations with the feudal lords," which is about assigning tasks, confirming the advice. This is an affirmative answer appearing in the *Image*. Based on this reading, I decided to work with an editor.

Will I be allowed by Princeton University Press to reproduce material from the Wilhelm/Baynes translation in my book?

All the interpretations presented in this book are based on the Wilhelm/Baynes translation. I thought my interpretations would be more solid if they included the original texts from that book. So I contacted the publisher, Princeton University Press, and requested permission to reproduce these texts.

Trying to predict their response, I asked the above question. The Hexagrams I obtained were 46, "Pushing Upward," effort, improving, boosting and 8, "Holding Together," union, jointly, in agreement, solid. Therefore, the *theme of the reading* is: *"Make an effort to be in*

[5] Feudal estates

agreement so the interpretations can be more solid," clearly confirming my belief.

The *Image* of Hexagram 8 gives the answer: "Thus the kings of antiquity bestowed the different states as fiefs and cultivated friendly relations with the feudal lords." This suggested that my request would be granted but subject to their authority, that is, under certain conditions.

Line 2 says, "If one is sincere, it furthers one to bring even a small offering," which implied that a fee would be required.

A week later I received the grant of permission involving a fee upon the publication of my book and limiting the total number of words from the original material and the percentage of original material in my book. So I made sure that my manuscript complied with the requirements.

What type of work should I pursue now?

Alicia had been working as a technician and also doing administrative work at a high-tech company. However, due to personal disagreements with some co-workers, she was told her position would be terminated.

She was anxious to know what type of work she should be pursuing next. She obtained Hexagram 7, "The Army," fighting for, struggle, campaign, and Hexagram 32, "Duration," staying the course, persistence.

By combining both meanings the *theme of the reading* is: *"Fight for your rights (sue the company. Your campaign (job search, will require persistence. Stay the course."*

Line 3 says, "Perchance the army carries corpses in the wagon. Misfortune." This *Line* refers to an unfortunate situation, in this case, the loss of her job. *Line* 4 says, "The army retreats. No blame." This *Line* refers not just to withdrawing, but to doing so in the most convenient terms.

The *Image* in Hexagram 32 says, "The superior man does not change his direction," which advises to seek similar type of work. This is the answer.

The *Image* in Hexagram 7 says, "The superior man increases his masses by generosity toward the people." This may refer to a very good settlement with her former employer. It also implies being hired and helping people.

Alicia sued the company for discrimination and, as a result, received a large severance payment. Then she embarked on a long and difficult job search. Eventually, she found an administrative position at a major university assisting students.

Was that operation really necessary?

After having a heart attack because of obstructed arteries leading to his heart, Jack was advised by his cardiologist to undergo a balloon angioplasty in which stents were inserted in some arteries to open them up. Immediately after this surgical procedure, he asked the above question.

He obtained Hexagram 46, "Pushing Upward," pumping and Hexagram 18, "Work on what has been spoiled," repairing, fixing, streamlining, healing.

Combining both meanings forms this *theme*: *"The pumping system (arteries) has been repaired,"* which describes the operation, a favorable sign.

Line 6 says, "Pushing upward in darkness. It furthers one to be unremittingly persevering." This translates to *"Not knowing for sure if this operation will correct the problem permanently, persist in doing checkups and making lifestyle changes (to prevent this problem from recurring)."* This completes the answer, which is positive but qualified.

As a consequence, he started a program of regular exercise and a healthier diet. A few years later, another artery became obstructed and the same operation was performed.

Can I expect to receive the payment that is now due?

Sharon loaned a large sum of money to be repaid in installments. Normally she would receive the payments by the 5th of each month. Yet nothing happened by the 8th of the current month, so she became concerned. So she asked the above question.

She obtained only Hexagram 59, "Dispersion," which in this case means "traveling far away." The *Judgment* says, "It furthers one to cross the great water. Perseverance furthers," which is favorable because it means that something is traveling to its destination. The *Image* says, "The kings of old sacrificed to the Lord and built temples." A sacrifice refers to a payment. Consider-ing the resulting texts, the *theme* is: *"The payment is traveling from a long distance."* The question was answered indirectly but affirmatively by all the parts of the result. A few days later, the payment arrived.

What should I do about my deficient computer?

Brenda's computer was not working well. She was not sure whether to have it repaired or buy a new one, which at that time was a costly alternative. Her question was: **"What is the best decision regarding my computer?"** She obtained Hexagram 64, "Before Completion," not completely and Hexagram 6, "Conflict," trouble. Obviously, the *theme of the reading* is descriptive: *"By not working completely well, your computer, is causing trouble."*

Line 5 says, "Perseverance brings good fortune. No remorse. The light of the superior man is true. Good fortune." This refers to keeping her computer and finding a competent technician.

The *Image* of Hexagram 64 says, "The superior man is careful in the differentiation of things, so that each finds its place." This is about someone capable of sorting things out or solving problems.

The *Image* of Hexagram 6 says, "Thus in all transactions the superior man carefully considers the beginning." This means that she needed to have a prior agreement with the technician about the cost before any repairs were made. Brenda decided to have her computer repaired.

Readings That Give a Weak Answer

Should I choose another preschool for my son?

Andrew was considering another preschool for his three-year old son, Peter, because of his slow speech development. He suspected Peter's current learning environment was causing the problem.

So he asked the above question. The result consisted of Hexagram 36, "Darkening of the light," hidden, latent and Hexagram 55, "Abundance," plenty. So the *theme* formed with both Hexagrams is: *"From latent to abundant,"* or *"What is latent should become abundant,"* which describes the current and the future situation.

The *Image* of Hexagram 55 says, "Thus the superior man decides lawsuits and carries out punishments." This is about making an important decision. The answer is in *Line* 4 of Hexagram 36: "One gets at the very heart of the darkening of the light, and leaves gate and courtyard."

According to the Wilhelm/Baynes book, this is about discovering the root of the problem and leaving, which advises to place Peter in another preschool. This is an affirmative answer. Andrew followed this advice and as a result, his son made remarkable progress.

Should I teach this class?

Raymond was a community college instructor who taught computer courses. Due to low enrollment, he was asked by the department chair to teach a class of a different type, "Technical Drawing," which he had studied a long time ago in college.

Concerned about his ability to teach that course, he inquired the above question. The result consisted only of

Hexagram 29, "The Abysmal," risk, danger. This Hexagram provided the *theme of the reading*: *"It is risky to teach something not totally familiar to you,"* describing the situation.

The *Judgment* and the *Image* are positive. The *Judgment* says, "If you are sincere, you have success in your heart, and whatever you do succeeds." The *Image* says, significantly, "The superior man walks in lasting virtue and carries on the business of teaching."

This is an affirmative answer. It says that in spite of the risks involved, if Raymond was truly dedicated he could succeed. So he accepted the offer and was able to teach the class without any problem.

Can I expect to be allowed to stay in this house for at least two more years?

Donna was concerned about possibly having to leave the house she was renting at some point in the future so she asked the above question. She obtained Hexagram 25, "Innocence (The Unexpected)," unexpectedly, beyond one's control, for no reason, and Hexagram 20, "Contemplation," considering, inspecting. Put together, both Hexagrams form the following *theme*: *"Due to reasons beyond your control, you will be considering (other houses for residence)."* Notice that this *theme* is not about staying.

Line 1 says, "Innocent behavior brings good fortune." This *Line* says that she should relax because she had done nothing wrong.

Line 4 says, "He who can be persevering remains without blame." By taking "persevering" as "staying," this *Line* advised Donna to stay at the current house as long as possible. The answer is a qualified yes, with the emphasis on the need to look for another place in the future.

The *Image* of Hexagram 20 says, "Thus the kings of old visited the regions of the world, contemplated the people, and gave them instruction." This might refer to visiting houses, getting to know the landlords, and explaining that she had a very good record as a tenant.

Two years and nine months later Donna was informed that her lease would expire so she had to look for another place.

Is this financial software a good tool for me to increase my wealth?

On the spur of the moment, Sharon bought a costly software package for making money by buying and selling stocks. Since she had a week to change her mind and return it, she asked the above question.

She obtained Hexagram 45, "Gathering Together," acquiring, amassing, collecting. The *theme* of this reading was obviously *"Acquired."* It did not advise buying the software; it simply stated the current situation because the purchase was already made.

The meaning "amassing" indicates that the product could be used to amass wealth. The *Image* says, "The superior man renews his weapons in order to meet the unforeseen." This is a warning about the work that would be required in order to deal with unknown situations." In other words, the software was a good tool but would take dedication and the results could not be always guaranteed.

The result actually answered two questions: whether the product was good and what Sharon could expect from it. A more pointed question would be: **"Should I keep this product?,"** which she asked next.

Should I keep this financial software?

This time Sharon obtained again Hexagram 45, "Gathering Together," acquiring and Hexagram 21, "Biting Through," hurdle, difficult. The *theme* is: *"You already acquired it and it will be difficult for you to use it,"* which reinforced the message already given in the *Image* of Hexagram 45.

The answer emphasized the difficulty of using this product rather than its usefulness. So it was a rather negative answer. Since Sharon didn't want to spend too much time analyzing stocks, she decided to return it. (Note: Although this reading has a negative answer and belongs in the next chapter, it is included here for continuity with the previous reading.)

What will it take for me to achieve peace and wisdom and be ready for my death?

This question was posed by John, 77 years old, as he was trying to make sense of the rest of his life. He obtained Hexagram 19, "Approach," approaching, getting closer and Hexagram 24, "Return." The *theme* formed by these Hexagrams is: *"You are approaching the time to return to where you came from."*

Line 2 says, "Joint approach. Good fortune. Everything furthers." The commentary to this *Line* says that the stimulus to approach comes from a high place, that is, he was being inspired to ask this question.

The *Image* of Hexagram 19 says, "The superior man is inexhaustible in his will to teach, and without limits in his tolerance and protection of the people." That was the answer he needed. He knew precisely what to do and the people he would be assisting.

What would be my best response when I am asked why I never got married?

Charles, a man in his fifties, had been asked why he never got married by every woman he dated. He wasn't sure why and also wanted to know the best possible answer. He obtained Hexagram 51, "The Arousing (Shock, Thunder)," arising, agitation, hectic, shock, and Hexagram 36, "Darkening of the Light," unclear, obscuring, hiding. The *theme* formed by the Hexagrams is: "*A hectic life and agitated mind (aggravated by the highly demanding and unstable jobs he held in the past) obscured his discernment and wisdom and didn't let him see all his possibilities.*" That made sense to Charles. It explained why he went into wrong relationships.

The *Image* in Hexagram 51 says, "Thus in fear and trembling the superior man sets his life in order and examines himself." This was advice for Charles to take a hard look at his life and his approach for finding a partner.

The *Image* in Hexagram 36 says, "Thus does the superior man live with the great mass. He veils his light, yet still shines." This seems to indicate that he did not have to explain everything when asked this question. Instead, he could choose what to say and how to say it in order to come across in the most positive way. That was the answer he needed.

Line 3 says, "Shock comes and makes one distraught. If shock spurs to action, one remains free of misfortune." This is about dealing with an uncomfortable situation by taking the initiative and acting appropriately. *Line* 4 says, "Shock is mired." This says that Charles should be able to minimize his anxiety or other people's surprise. As a result of this reading, Charles was able to answer this question with self-confidence.

Should my website include a blog?

Having decided to create a website to describe and promote this book, I was not sure whether it would be really necessary to include a blog in it and incur the extra cost. So I asked the above question. The result consisted of Hexagram 1, "The Creative," creativity, activity, and Hexagram 3, "Difficulty at the Beginning," creating. So the *theme of the reading* is: *"Use your creativity to produce (content)."*

Line 3 says, "All day long the superior man is creatively active," which is about constant activity. So the result is about constantly creating content, which refers to a blog, because the rest of a website is usually static.

Line 6 says, "Arrogant dragon will have cause to repent," warning against losing touch with people and becoming isolated.

The *Judgment* of Hexagram 3 confirms that warning: "Furthering through perseverance. Nothing should be undertaken. (This phrase is irrelevant because the *theme* is about activity.) It furthers one to appoint helpers." In the context of the *theme*, this is advice to accept people's input or help in designing the blog.

Should I retire now or continue working for another year?

Roxanne had a choice to retire, with the consequent loss of income, or stay for another year in a job that she loved but was stressful and often required very long hours.

When she asked the above question, the result was Hexagram 44, "Coming to Meet," finding, meeting a need, and Hexagram 28, "Preponderance of the Great," unbalanced, unbearable, unsustainable. Putting both Hexagrams together, the following theme is formed: "Find something that meets your needs so you can avoid an unsustainable and unbearable situation."

The Image of Hexagram 28 says: "The superior man, when he stands alone, is unconcerned, and if he has to renounce the world, is undaunted," advice to retire and not worry. Line 6 says: "He comes to meet with his horns. Humiliation. No blame." This is a warning about bad consequences to Roxanne's health if she continued working at the same pace. Roxanne decided to retire and, at the right time, look for a part-time job that would be fulfilling and, along with her pension, would satisfy her financial needs.

Is it best for me to get a part-time job as a resource specialist?

Roxanne was already retired and was considering getting a part-time job similar to the full-time job she had before. The response she got to this question consisted of Hexagram 51, "The Arousing (Shock, Thunder)" and Hexagram 16, "Enthusiasm," love.

The first Hexagram stands in this case for awakening and becoming aware. Putting both hexagrams together forms this *theme*: "*Be aware of some jobs you may be enthusiastic about.*" This response does not directly answer the question because it's not about getting (a job). It is about making Roxanne aware that there were other jobs available that she would also love to do.

Line 1 is positive about those jobs.

A Lost-and-Found Story

I misplaced the keys to my house and could not find them in any of the usual places. I was concerned that I might have dropped them somewhere while running errands. So I did the three following readings.

Will I be able to find my keys?

I obtained Hexagram 24, "Return," recovery, and Hexagram 2, "The Receptive," receiving.

Readings That Give a Weak Answer

Where should I look for my keys?

I obtained Hexagram 19, "Approach," coming up, and Hexagram 11, "Peace," harmony, good. I didn't understand this result yet, see explanation below.

Should I look for my keys actively?

I obtained Hexagram 5, "Waiting," patience, and again Hexagram 11, "Peace," harmony, good.

The next morning, my guest found the keys in the dryer and brought them to me, confirming the first and third reading. I realized that I had put my jacket in the dryer because it was soaked by the rain and the keys were in one of its pockets.

Reviewing the second reading, the two Trigrams in Hexagram 19 are "lake" at the bottom, which is equivalent to Hexagram 58, representing humidity, and "receptive" at the top, cavity, which is equivalent to Hexagram 2, which represents a space. That was a good hint.

IX. Readings That Give a Negative Answer

Usually, a negative answer is denoted by a general statement, a result in which a) neither the *theme* nor any resulting text answers the question asked or b) the *theme* is unrelated or opposed to the question, the surrounding situation, or the main issue. This *disconnection* can be interpreted, depending on the question, as "no," "nothing is happening," "do nothing," "no results," "it does not matter," etc. Notice that the *disconnection* could be subtle, and may occur even if the resulting Hexagrams are individually positive, like Hexagram 1, 14, 42, etc.

As the following readings show, a negative answer is not necessarily unfavorable because it may suggest a new perspective. To confirm that this is the case, it is advisable to *cross-check* the reading with a new one by asking a more pointed question or a question from another angle. The new reading may give the final answer.

Planning a trip to India

Clarence had a very active life and was thinking about taking a trip to India but was not sure if it would be a good idea, considering his physical condition and the fact that he was 86 years old. So he asked, **"Will I be in good condition to go to India in a few months?"**

He obtained Hexagram 51, "The Arousing," hectic, agitation and Hexagram 54, "The Marrying Maiden," engaged in, busy with. By combining the most relevant meanings the following *theme* can be formed: "*Given the hectic activity that you are engaged in,*" which can also be expressed as: "*You are engaged in hectic activity.*"

This result is not about traveling so it is a negative answer. It suggests that Clarence was too active given his condition, a negative sign. Moreover, *Line* 2 in Hexagram 51 says, "You lose your treasures. Do not go in pursuit of them. After seven days you will get them back again." In other words, it counsels patience in regard to this trip.

The *Image* of Hexagram 51 says, "The superior man sets his life in order and examines himself," which refers to taking a hard look at his fast-paced life and having a medical examination. The text of the *Image* of Hexagram 54 says, "The superior man understands the transitory in the light of the eternity of the end," which says: "the trip is transitory, put first things first." This is a negative indirect answer recommending a postponement. To confirm this result, Clarence asked the following question.

Readings That Give a Negative Answer

What is the state of my health?

Clarence obtained Hexagram 62, "Preponderance of the Weak," exceeding, overdoing, going too far, and Hexagram 47, "Oppression (Exhaustion)," depletion. By combining both meanings this *theme* is formed: *"If you go beyond your limits, you'll deplete your health."*

The second *Line* says, "He does not reach his prince and meets the official. No blame." This advises to exercise restraint. The third *Line* says, "If one is not extremely careful, somebody may come up from behind and strike him," which warns about the consequences of being careless.

The fifth *Line* says, "The prince shoots and hits him who is in the cave." This positive *Line* says that Clarence could still attain his goal.

The *Image* of Hexagram 47 says, "Thus the superior man stakes his life on following his will." This *text* advised him to pursue his goals.

Taking the texts into account, the whole answer is: *"Despite your delicate condition, if you are careful and know how to pace yourself, you can fulfill your heart's desire,"* which goes beyond answering the original question.

Based on these readings, Clarence decided to postpone his trip to India. He took the trip a few years later. (Note: This reading has a weak positive answer but is placed here for continuity.)

What will be the result of my job interview yesterday?

Alice just had an interview and was told that a decision would be made in three weeks. Since she didn't want to waste her time waiting, she asked the above question to the *I Ching*.

The result consisted of only Hexagram 31, "Influence (Wooing)," interested, calling forth, requesting, applying for. So the *theme* is: "*You were interested, were called for an interview, and applied for the job.*"

The *theme* simply describes the current situation, with no further outcome. The *Image* says, "Thus the superior man encourages people to approach him by his readiness to receive them."

The *Judgment* says, "Influence, success. To take a maiden to wife brings good fortune." Although this text seems to indicate a hiring, it is only advice to the employer to hire someone. To clarify this result, Alice asked the next question.

Will there be a job offer at this time?

Alice obtained Hexagram 1, "The Creative," creativity, being active and Hexagram 10, "Treading," proceeding one step at a time.

Line 3 says, "All day long the superior man is creatively active. At nightfall his mind is still beset with cares. Danger. No Blame."

The *Image* of Hexagram 1 says, "The superior man makes himself strong and untiring." The *Image* of Hexagram 10 says, "Thus the superior man discriminates between high and low and thereby fortifies the thinking of the people."

This whole answer can be summed up as *"Be active, creative, untiring, and discriminating in order to proceed one step at a time and see what results you are getting."*

This answer is not about being offered a job. It is a *general statement* on how to conduct a job search successfully, so the answer was negative. Alice didn't get the job.

Shall I take this apartment?

Sherri had been looking for an apartment to rent for some time. She finally found an attractive unit but it was very highly priced. Undecided, she asked the above question, She obtained Hexagram 53, "Gradual Development," process, and Hexagram 14, "Possessions in Great Measure," place, having. By combining both meanings, the *theme of the reading* is: *"You are going through a process to find the right place."*

This is a negative answer because it's not about taking the apartment. *Line* 1 says, "The wild goose gradually draws near the shore," *Line* 2 says, "The wild goose gradually draws near the cliff," *Line* 4 says, "The wild goose gradually draws near the tree," and *Line* 5 says, "The wild goose draws near the summit. For three years the woman has no child. In the end nothing can hinder her. Good fortune."

The *Lines* indicate different stages of a process which would be finally successful. None of them advises to take any action. Therefore, the answer was: *"Do nothing about this apartment. Continue the search."* Eventually, Sherri found a satisfactory place.

Will the class I want to teach get enough students?

Al was a community college instructor. His class would take place the following semester only if a sufficient number of students enrolled in it. Otherwise, it would be cancelled. Since he wanted to predict his future situation, he asked the above question.

He obtained Hexagram 34, "The Power of the Great," empowered, authorized, and Hexagram 64, "Before Completion," incomplete, not enough, insufficient. The combination of both symbols produced this *theme*: *"You were authorized to teach that class but there will not be enough students enrolled."* This is a direct negative answer.

Line 1 says, "Power in the toes. Continuing brings misfortune." *Line* 3 says, "A goat butts against a hedge and gets its horns entangled." *Line* 6 says, "A goat butts against a hedge. It cannot go backward, it cannot go forward." These three *Line*s refer to Al not being able to proceed, confirming the *theme of the reading*. The class was cancelled on the first day due to low enrollment.

Avoiding False Expectations

Greg met Cathy at a party and felt very attracted to her. After having a nice conversation, he asked her for her phone number and said he would call her in a few days. When he got home, he had some doubts. Not wanting to have false expectations, he consulted the *I Ching*.

His question was: **"What should I expect when I call Cathy later on?"** He obtained Hexagram 24, "Return," getting back and Hexagram 51, "The Arousing," shock, becoming aware, realizing. The *theme of the reading* is: "*When you get back to her you'll be shocked.*" It is not about finding receptivity or having any further communication.

In addition, *Line* 4 in Hexagram 24 says, "Walking in the midst of others, one returns alone." This is not about meeting either. The *Image* in Hexagram 51 says, "The superior man sets his life in order and examines himself." This could have been advice for Greg to do a self-examination and pay more attention to his feelings when meeting someone.

Not being sure that he understood the answer, Greg decided to call Cathy anyway to find out one way or the other. After all, he figured, it would be foolish to miss an opportunity because of a negative reading. He only got a recording and never received a call back, which was an unpleasant surprise.

Should I take this supplement for my fatigue?

Bill had been feeling tired and with low energy lately. An acquaintance recommended an antioxidant supplement that would energize him by oxygenating the cells in his body. So he asked the above question.

He obtained Hexagram 64, "Before Completion," not quite, not totally, insufficient and Hexagram 38, "Opposition," against, discrimination. The *theme* formed with these symbols is: *"It's not quite what you need, don't take it. Use discrimination."*

Line 1 in Hexagram 64 says, "He gets his tail in the water. Humiliation." It advises to hold back and avoid reckless actions. The *Image* here says, "The superior man is careful in the differentiation of things, so that each finds its place." This is advice to sort out and clarify things.

The *Image* in Hexagram 38 says, "Thus amid all fellowship the superior man retains his individuality." This is about seeking an individualized solution or treatment. Realizing that he had not asked the essential question, he did the following reading.

Why am I feeling tired?

Bill obtained Hexagram 37, "The Family," household, domestic, and Hexagram 20,"Contemplation," seeing, being seen, examining. By putting them together, this *theme* is formed: "*Your domestic life needs to be examined.*"

Line 1 in Hexagram 37 says, "Firm seclusion within the family. Remorse disappears." It advises to retire and get enough rest. *Line* 3 says, "When tempers flare up in the family, too great severity brings remorse. Good fortune nonetheless." This says that in doubtful instances, it is preferable to be exceedingly thorough and careful.

The *Image* in this Hexagram says, "The superior man has substance in his words and duration in his way of life." This refers to the knowledge and expertise of a doctor. The *Image* in Hexagram 20 says, "The kings of old visited the regions of the world, contemplated the people, and gave them instruction." This refers to seeing a doctor and getting advice.

Readings That Give a Negative Answer

This is an instance of a weak answer because the answer is not expressed by the *theme* but is implied in *Line* 1. After seeing a doctor, Bill found out that the reason for his fatigue was a sleeping disorder called sleep apnea. (Because this reading has a weak answer it belongs in Chapter VIII. It is included here for continuity with the previous reading.)

An Impossible Business Arrangement

Teresa had a chain of spas in Mexico and wanted to expand her business into the United States. Since Vera had a similar business in the States, Teresa invited Vera to visit her town and stay at her home as her guest. Teresa's plan was to get into a business relationship in which Vera would act as her representative in America, introducing some of Teresa's products there.

So she spent all her time entertaining Vera while sacrificing her own business and family life. Although Vera enjoyed her stay very much, she balked every time Teresa tried to discuss a possible business relationship. Teresa was losing her patience. She wanted to know if her effort would pay off.

So Teresa asked, **"How could I persuade Vera to get into a business arrangement?"** She obtained Hexagram 41, "Decrease," sacrifices, expenses and Hexagram 26, "The Taming Power of the Great," holding back. So the *themes of the reading* are: "*You are making sacrifices and she is holding back*" and "*You are making sacrifices, hold back.*" These *themes* are not about an evolving relationship.

Line 3 says, "When three people journey together, their number decreases by one, when one man journeys alone, he finds a companion." This suggests that what is excessive, like entertaining Vera, would not work, but simply following her own path would naturally attract the right clients.

The *Image* in Hexagram 41 says, appropriately, "Thus the superior man controls his anger and restrains his instincts." The *Image* Hexagram 26 says, "Thus the superior man acquaints himself with many deeds of the past, in order to strengthen his character thereby." This says, *"take this situation as a learning experience."*

Is there a potential for a long-term relationship between Will and me?

Marie's boyfriend, Will, wanted to marry her. Although he was very committed to her, she was not sure that he was the right person for a long-term relationship. So she asked the above question.

She obtained Hexagram 36, "Darkening of the Light," hiding, not showing, which is the *theme of the reading*. The message here is not about a long-lasting relationship but about things Will hid from Marie, so the answer is negative.

The *Image* says, "He veils his light, yet still shines." In other words, *"although Will had not shown some aspects of his personality, he was sincere and had good qualities."* The *Judgment* says, "In adversity, it furthers one to be persevering." In view of the discouraging *theme* and the word "adversity," this might read: *"You are dissatisfied. Keep seeking the relationship that you want."*

Eventually, Marie noticed some of Will's habits, like his addiction to food and drink, which were very annoying to her. After having several discussions with Will, she realized that it would be quite difficult for him to change his behavior, so she eventually ended the relationship.

Will I be selected to serve as a juror?

Michael received a summons for jury service and **wanted to predict whether he would be selected to serve as a juror.** He obtained Hexagram 31, "Influence," summons, citation and Hexagram 43, "Breakthrough," announcing. By combining them, the *theme* is: "*The citation has been announced,*" which describes the current situation.

Line 1 says, "The influence shows itself in the big toe." According to the comment in the Wilhelm/Baynes book, this is about an influence that was not important and did not have any visible effect. *Line* 2 says, "Tarrying brings good fortune." This means that a delay would be advisable.

The *Image* of Hexagram 43 says, "The superior man dispenses riches downward and refrains from resting on his virtue." This is about leniency from the court. This result ignored the question and advised Michael to request a postponement. Since he was due for a cardiac examination in a few days, Michael requested a postponement of the jury service until his heart condition was diagnosed.

Shall I pursue pottery as a profession?

Maria loved pottery. She took workshops and spent hours working by herself at a studio and producing beautiful work. She wanted to know if she could do pottery professionally, so she asked the above question.

She obtained Hexagram 13, "Fellowship with Men," friend, amateur and Hexagram 25, "Innocence (The Unexpected," spontaneously, without ulterior motives. The *theme of the reading* is not about a career. It says: *"As an amateur, you can do pottery without any ulterior motives, that is, not for profit."* That was confirmed by the fact that Maria was not able to sell anything so far.

The *Image* of Hexagram 13 says, "Thus the superior man organizes the clans and makes distinctions between things." The *Image* of Hexagram 25 says, "Thus the kings of old, rich in virtue, and in harmony with the time, fostered and nourished all beings." These two texts could indicate a profession that is about organizing, coordinating, or educating.

A Career Decision

Monica, a married young woman, quit a very demanding job at a big consulting firm that left her exhausted. She wanted to work under different conditions and wondered what type of company would be most suitable to her.

After a brief discussion with me, she categorized the possible companies in three types: big, startup, and non-profit. Then she asked: **"What type of company should I consider for my next job?"**

The result consisted of Hexagrams 54, "The Marrying Maiden" and 40, "Deliverance." The *applicable meanings* are commitment and employment for the first symbol and exiting, becoming free for the second. So the *theme of the reading* is: "*In your employment you should be able to be free.*" The first *Line* of Hexagram 54 says, "The marrying maiden as a concubine. A lame man who is able to tread. Undertakings bring good fortune." This is not about quitting. It is about taking a subordinate position that can still be rewarding. This result is not about any of the three alternatives mentioned above. It suggests a better alternative: employment with freedom. Monica found a job with flexible hours at a big high-tech company.

Is there any urgency to sell my property?

Richard, who resided in Florida, needed to sell his house in Mexico City. Eventually, he was contacted by a prospective buyer with a reasonable offer. Anxious to close the transaction, he accepted a down payment and planned a trip to Mexico to complete the sale without realizing that he would be greatly inconvenienced by having to be absent from his workplace and cancel important commitments.

Having second thoughts about the urgency of the transaction, he asked the above question. He obtained Hexagram 34, "The Power of the Great," power, capability, being able, being forced, and Hexagram 63, "After Completion," completed, done. The *theme* they form is not about urgency. It basically says, *"You have the power to complete the transaction."*

Line 2 in Hexagram 34 says, "Perseverance brings good fortune." In other words, persist with the sale. *Line* 4 says, "Perseverance brings good fortune. Remorse dis-appears. The hedge opens; there is no entanglement. Power depends upon the axle of a big cart." This may refer to completing the sale. *Line* 5 says, "Loses the goat with ease. No remorse." This is about flexibility, possibly on the part of the buyer. The *theme, "You are forced to complete the transaction"* does not apply here because two of the *lines* are about using his power and the other is about flexibility.

The *Image* of Hexagram 34 says, "Thus the superior man does not tread upon paths that do not accord with established order." This refers to the buyer respecting his previous commitment. Based on this reading, Richard postponed his trip until a more convenient time and the buyer did not object to the delay.

He was glad that he did not purchase any other property

After selling his property in Mexico City, Richard wanted to know if it would be wise to use the money to buy a house he had seen in another town. So he asked, **"Is it preferable to purchase another property with this money?"**

He obtained Hexagram 3, "Difficulty at the Beginning," just created, at the beginning, and Hexagram 33, "Retreat," sending away from, recession. The *theme* is: *"The amount you just made from the sale should be sent away. There will be a recession."* It is definitely not about purchasing.

Readings That Give a Negative Answer

Line 1 says, "Hesitation and hindrance. It furthers one to remain persevering. It furthers one to appoint helpers." This advises to get professional advice before taking any action.

Line 3 says, "Whoever hunts deer without the forester only loses his way in the forest. The superior man understands the signs of the time and prefers to desist. To go on brings humiliation." This is a warning against acting without guidance.

Line 4 says, "Horse and wagon part. Strive for union. To go brings good fortune." This could refer to parting with the money to invest it productively.

Line 6 says, "Horse and wagon part. Bloody tears flow." This could be a warning against making a wrong investment and losing money.

The *Image* in Hexagram 3 says, "Thus the superior man brings order out of confusion." This could be advice to be clear about the possible investment options. To confirm this interpretation, Richard asked the following question.

What should I do now with the money from the sale of my property?

Richard obtained Hexagram 53, "Development (Gradual Progress," growth, and Hexagram 8, "Holding Together," keeping. The *theme* here is: "*While your funds are growing they should be kept under your control.*"

The *Image* in Hexagram 8 says, "Thus the kings of antiquity bestowed the different states as fiefs and cultivated friendly relations with the feudal lords." This could mean diversifying investments.

Line 3 says, "The wild goose gradually draws near the plateau. The man goes forth and does not return. The woman carries a child but does not bring it forth. Misfortune. It furthers one to fight off robbers." This is an advice to choose gradual growth over unreliable schemes.

Line 6 says, "The wild goose gradually draws near the cloud heights. Its feathers can be used for the sacred dance. Good fortune." This refers to getting good results in the end. The *Image* of Hexagram 53 says, "Thus the superior man abides in dignity and virtue in order to improve the mores." This is about taking time to learn about the best investing possibilities.

As a result of this reading, Richard invested in foreign currencies and commodities. A few months later the house prices started a dramatic decline due to the subprime mortgage crisis, triggering a severe recession, as hinted by the previous reading. (Note: This reading has a strong positive answer but has been placed here for continuity with the previous reading.

How should I decide about this expensive orthodontic work?

This reading shows that a negative answer could also be advice to take a new course of action. Henry was unable to have a full smile because of excessive tissue on top of his upper lip. He felt this was affecting his social life by making him appear too serious. An orthodontist suggested that using corrective braces for a year would eventually expand the upper gum and expose his front teeth 2 mm more upon smiling.

Readings That Give a Negative Answer

Unsure about having such a small and slow modification at a price he considered excessive, he consulted the *I Ching* about the wisdom of undergoing that treatment by asking the above question. He obtained Hexagram 41, "Decrease," reducing, shortening, expenses, cost, and Hexagram 11, "Peace," harmony, fair, balanced.

One *theme* formed by these Hexagrams is: *"The cost should be reduced to be fair."* There is no reference in the result to "expanding," which is what the treatment would have done. Based on this negative answer he informed the dentist that he could not afford the price and canceled the treatment.

Hoping to get a lower price, Henry went to see another orthodontist who in turn referred him to a cosmetic surgeon. This specialist mentioned a simpler operation by which the tissue above his upper lip would be cut and reduced, at a much smaller cost.

Henry went back to the original reading and realized that there was another valid *theme*: *"Shortening (the tissue, brings harmony."* *Line* 3 in Hexagram 41 says, "When three people journey together, their number decreases by one. When one person journeys alone, he finds a companion." This implies that the excessive needs to be reduced and the simple will work fine. This could refer to the price or to the type of treatment.

The *Image* of Hexagram 11 says, "Thus the ruler divides and completes the course of heaven and earth; he furthers and regulates the gifts of heaven and earth, and so aids the people." This says that there was a convenient treatment available. So Henry went to the cosmetic surgeon that for a much smaller price cut and reduced the tissue above the upper lip, which solved the problem.

Had he *cross-checked* the initial reading with another reading by asking **Should I seek another treatment?**, it would have been easier for him to confirm that the result of the initial reading was also about seeking the other type of treatment.

Is there a possibility for this relationship to work out?

Alejandro met Carmen during one of his trips to Brazil and fell instantly in love with her. When he was back in his native country, Argentina, he corresponded with her on a regular basis. He felt that he had found the love of his life.

However, during his stays at Carmen's home, he was not totally accepted by her grown-up children, who were still living with her. Because of them, Carmen was never totally available to him.

Since she professed to love him, Alejandro tried to work out a solution and eventually threatened to leave her unless she spend more time with him. Unwilling to break up the relationship, Carmen went to Argentina to visit Alejandro several times, but would never commit to staying with him on a permanent basis.

Trying to clarify the situation, Alejandro asked the above question to an *I Ching* reader. He obtained Hexagram 64, "Before Completion," incomplete, not quite and Hexagram 29, "The Abysmal," dangerous, unfortunate. The *theme of the reading* is: *"An incomplete relationship will be unfortunate,"* describing the current state of the relationship and the unfavorable future.

Line 4 says, "Shock, to discipline the Devil's Country. For three years, great awards are awarded." This is about the need to constantly warn Carmen. *Line* 5 says, "Perseverance brings good fortune. No remorse." This seems to refer to a period of harmony. *Line* 6 says, "There is drinking of wine in genuine confidence. No blame. But if one wets his head, he loses it, in truth." This was an ominous warning.

In other words, *"don't celebrate too soon because things may revert to their previous condition."* Realizing that there was no future in the relationship, Alejandro eventually ended the relationship.

Should I change my business card now?

Jim started a new occupation as a business and career consultant while still working at his current profession. He considered getting a new business card, but was not yet ready to be seen differently by many people who would relate to him in his current capacity. That was his dilemma.

In response to the above question, he obtained Hexagram 19, "Approach," approaching, bringing up a subject, and Hexagram 36, "Darkening of the Light," hiding, not showing.

By combining both Hexagrams, he obtained this *theme*: *"Know how to approach people and bring up what you do, so you won't have to show a new business card."*

The *Judgment* of Hexagram 19 says, "When the eighth month comes there will be misfortune." This may imply that eventually the current business card would not be useful anymore and a new one would be necessary.

The *Image* of Hexagram 19 says, "Thus the superior man is inexhaustible in his will to teach, and without limits in his tolerance and protection of the people."

The *Image* in Hexagram 36 says, "Thus does the superior man live with the great mass. He veils his light, yet still shines." This may refer to using discretion and tact when talking about his work.

Line 2 in Hexagram 19 says, "Joint approach. Good fortune. Everything furthers." This indicates that Jim needed to see sufficient interest from other people before explaining his new type of work."

Line 3 says, "Comfortable approach. Nothing that would further. If one is induced to grieve over it, one becomes free of blame." This is advice to be more active and approach more people. There is no reference to making any immediate change. Jim kept his business card for the time being.

Considering the pros — business growth and expanding my network — and the cons — cost and time involved — would it be advisable to join this business networking group?

Anthony was a financial consultant and had to decide whether or not to join a business networking group he had been attending on an informal basis. The Hexagrams he obtained were 33, "Retreat," stepping back, and 32, "Duration," staying the course, preserving, long-term.

There is no reference in this result to "investing" or to "joining," so this is a negative answer.

Readings That Give a Negative Answer

The *theme* that can be formed with these Hexagrams is: "*While stepping back, keep the informal connection and stay the course.*"

Line 2 says, "He holds him fast with yellow ox hide. No one can tear him loose." This refers to some ties that should be kept. *Line* 5 says, "Friendly retreat. Perseverance brings good fortune." This implies that despite stepping back, Anthony could still have a friendly connection.

Line 6 says, "Cheerful retreat. Everything serves to further." This says that despite stepping back, he could still benefit from the group. As a result, he did not join the business networking group but maintained the informal connection.

How can we persuade these people to sell us their mansion?

During a visit to Amsterdam, Caroline met Pieter, a very well-to-do Dutch lawyer and married him a year later, making The Netherlands her country of residence.

Since both of them had children from previous marriages, they decided to move to a larger house. She fell in love with a beautiful mansion in disrepair in a residential area of the city.

It belonged to a family from impoverished nobility that could not afford the upkeep. Caroline made several offers but the owners would not sell it. So she consulted an *I Ching* reader to inquire if there was any way to persuade the owners.

She obtained Hexagram 1, "The Creative," activity, causing, and Hexagram 44, "Coming to Meet," finding, meeting requirements, reaching a compromise.

Two possible *themes* are: *"If you are creative, you and the owners can reach a compromise"* and *"Through your activity you will find a house that meets your requirements."*

Line 1 implies the second *theme* because it says, "Hidden dragon, do not act." This is not about reaching a compromise but about something that is hidden that needs to be found, so no action could be taken yet.

The *Image* of Hexagram 44 says, "Thus does the prince act when disseminating his commands and proclaiming them to the four quarters of heaven," suggesting that houses for sale were widely advertised. Eventually, Caroline and Pieter found another house.

She replied to my message. Will this communication evolve favorably?

This reading has a negative answer even though the component Hexagrams in the result are individually positive. Todd sent a brief message to Janet, a woman he found through an online dating service.

After she responded in a very cordial manner, he wanted to predict how their communication would evolve. He obtained Hexagram 11, "Peace," harmony, a perfect match and Hexagram 5, "Waiting," awaiting, counting on, trusting.

Hexagram 11 does not relate to the current situation because Todd didn't know Janet. Moreover, Hexagram 5 is not about continuing the communication. The only meaningful *theme* these symbols can form is a *general statement*: *"There should be a perfect match so you should wait for it."*

Line 5 says: "The sovereign I gives his daughter in marriage. This brings blessing and good fortune." It is a favorable message, but in the context of the *theme,* it can only refer to a future possibility with someone else. To confirm this interpretation, Todd asked the next question.

Is there a possibility of a deep relationship between Janet and me?

The result consisted of Hexagram 25, "The Unexpected," surprise, having no expectations, spontaneous. The *theme* here is about not having any expectations and letting new situations arise spontaneously, confirming the previous reading. It ignores the question, so the answer is again negative.

Feeling unsure about his own interpretation, Todd opted to continue corresponding with Janet but after responding to her second message he didn't hear from her anymore.

Is it time for me to move from my present place?

Molly felt quite isolated living in a suburb in California. So she wanted to move to San Francisco, which she thought would be a more exciting place to live. She consulted an *I Ching* reader, who advised her to ask the above question.

The result was Hexagram 29, "The Abysmal," danger, and Hexagram 48, "The Well," source. *Line* 3 says, "In danger like this, pause first and wait. Otherwise you will fall into a pit in the abyss."

According to the *I Ching* reader, the *theme* is: *"In this depressed economy you have a source of income."*

There is no reference to "moving." This result reminded Molly of the bad existing economic situation and that she was lucky to have a good job only five minutes away from her home. Living far away in San Francisco would have made it harder for her to continue working at her current job or to find another. So she decided not to move for the time being.

Will I be successful if I start a new profession as a mind-body-spirit consultant?

Olga was a nurse and wanted to apply the knowledge she accumulated during many years into a consultancy or coaching practice. She obtained Hexagram 57, "The Gentle (The Penetrating, Wind," figuring out, and Hexagram 44, "Coming to Meet," finding, meeting, networking.

The *theme* is: *"You will have to figure out how to network to find clients."* There is a strong emphasis on advertising because both *Images* are about it. The *Image* in Hexagram 57 says, "Thus the superior man spreads his commands abroad and carries out his undertakings." And the *Image* in Hexagram 44 says, "Thus does the prince act when disseminating his commands and proclaiming them to the four quarters of heaven."

Line 4 in Hexagram 57 says, "Remorse vanishes. During the hunt three kinds of game are caught." This *Line* is about "hunting," that is, having the ability to get clients. The answer is negative because it does not answer the question, Moreover, the *theme* is about a requirement to do something she didn't feel like doing: getting clients by advertising his skills.

Olga decided to pursue the consulting practice only on a voluntary basis by assisting her friends and acquaintances. A better question would have been: **Given my present circumstances and my preferences, is it advisable for me to look for work as a mind-body-spirit consultant?**

Should I hurry to invest before the end of this year?

Jack, a retired senior citizen, didn't know much about investment options. He wanted to find a way to invest his money without having it tied up.

Some important changes could have happened to the economy in the year after the 2012 presidential election, so he wondered if he needed to act before the end of the year.

In response to the above question he obtained Hexagram 27, "Providing Nourishment," feeding, financing, investing, informing, educating and Hexagram 14, "Possession in Great Measure," money, assets, security.

Nothing in this result is about urgency, although it does encourage investing. One *theme* formed with these Hexagrams is: *"While investing in the economic activities that are important to you, you should have security."* That made a lot of sense to Jack. Another *theme* is: *"Educate yourself to find secure investments."*

Line 2 says, "To seek nourishment from the hill. Continuing to do this brings misfortune." This seems to say that Social Security and Jack's pensions, his current sources of income, would not provide sufficient security in the long run.

Line 3 says, "Turning away from nourishment. Perseverance brings misfortune." Some investments will not provide security. *Line* 4 says, "Turning to the summit for provision of nourishment brings good fortune." Interpreting "summit" as institutions, this *Line* says that there are some secure institutions where Jack could invest. To confirm this interpretation, Jack asked the following question.

How should I go about choosing investment options?

This reading is interpreted in light of the previous reading. The result consisted of Hexagram 56, "The Wanderer," exploring, and Hexagram 15, "Modesty," low, easy, accessible. The *theme* is: *"Explore the possible options, so your funds will be easily accessible. Growth will be modest."*

Line 4 says, "The wanderer rests in a shelter. He obtains his property and an ax. My heart is not glad." In other words, Jack's decision didn't have to be final. At some point he could switch to another option or consider diversification (mutual funds). Jack felt that he was ready to explore various possibilities. (Note: This reading has a strong positive answer but has been placed in this chapter for continuity with the previous reading. It applies only to Jack's situation.)

Readings That Give a Negative Answer

Will Scotland vote for independence in 2014?

This reading was done September 9, 2014. The Referendum took place September 18, with polls showing both sides almost evenly split. The result consisted of Hexagram 30, "The Clinging, Fire," and Hexagram 27, "Providing Nourishment," giving (concessions). The *theme of the reading* gives the answer: "*By clinging to the U.K., it will be given concessions.*"

This *theme* is not about separation. Confirming the result of this reading, just a few days before the vote, the British Prime Minister promised to give more powers to the Scottish Parliament. That could have persuaded enough voters to stay in the U.K.

Is it in my highest good to move out of the U.S.?

Lynn was retired and on fixed income and didn't think that her financial situation would allow her to live in America much longer given the high cost of living and inflation. So she seriously considered moving to a Latin American country where her retirement money would allow her to live within her means.

She obtained Hexagram 24, "Return," change your mind, remorse, turn back, and Hexagram 8, "Holding Together," being with. So the *theme* is: "*Turn back to be with your people.*" It contradicts the question.

Line 1 says: "Return from a short distance, no need for remorse." This is about turning back before it's too late.

Line 5 says: "Noble hearted return, no remorse." This line is a warning that says that if Lynn left, she would eventually return to the U.S.

The *Image* of Hexagram 8 says: "The kings of antiquity bestowed the different states as fiefs." This is about renting out one of Lynn's rooms to earn extra income.

How should I respond to my sister's invitation to attend her son's birthday party in New York?

That was a difficult decision for Robert to make since he had deadlines to meet but he also felt very close to his nephew.

He obtained Hexagram 45, "Gathering Together," joining, agreeing, and Hexagram 12, "Standstill," disconnection, apart.

Line 6 says: "Lamenting and sighing, flood of tears. No blame." This *Line* does not imply a visit but a regret.

The *Judgment* of Hexagram 45 says: *"The king approaches his temple."* Putting all together, the answer is *"Agree with your sister to not visiting this time but another time."*

X. How to Start Doing Readings

The intuitive approach introduced in this book facilitates the interpretation of readings and reveals clear answers to your questions. These are the main points of this approach:

Start by reading “Tossing the Coins and Building the Hexagrams,” Chapter I. Next, study some readings in Chapters VII, VIII, and IX. Then do a reading about a simple issue and avoid any preconceptions. Preferably, use an open-ended question, starting with: what, how, why, etc. See examples in Chapter V. Build the resulting Hexagram or Hexagrams, find the Hexagram number(s) using the Table on page 104, and find the *applicable meanings* in the Dictionary of the 64 Hexagrams.

Then observe the phrases that can be built with these meanings until you recognize the most significant phrase from among them, the *theme* of the reading. The *theme* often reveals the answer. In other cases, the *theme* relates to the surrounding situation or the main issue and provides a frame of reference for understanding the resulting texts—any moving *Lines, Images*, and *Judgments*—which may reveal the answer.

These texts can be found in the Wilhelm/Baynes classical translation, whose basic section is online at: www.pantherwebworks.com/I_Ching/.

However, if no answer is found in the resulting texts, it is implicitly negative but may suggest a new perspective. If the response is not clear to you, do another reading with a question that is more pointed or from another angle. *Understanding a reading will resonate with you!*

XI. Glossary

Answer - The information provided by the result of a reading in response to the question asked.

Applicable meanings - For a given reading, the meanings of the resulting Hexagram(s) that relate to the question that was asked, the present or future situation, or the main issue.

Cross-checking a reading - If the result of a reading is negative or seems obscure or ambiguous, it may be clarified by a new reading with a more pointed question or a question from another angle.

Great man - A term used in the *I Ching* to denote a wise person, a person of authority, a source of knowledge, or one's source of inspiration, inner wisdom, and intuition.

Holistic perception - Perception of the *big picture* in the result of a reading which is expressed by the *theme* of the reading. The *theme* provides a frame of reference for understanding the moving *Lines*, the *Images*, and the *Judgments*.

Interpretation - A result that has been interpreted.

Message - The information provided by the result of a reading, not necessarily answering the question asked.

Moving Line - A *Line* produced by three heads (full) or three tails (broken). For any given reading the *moving Line(s)* change into the opposite *Lines(s)* and the *static Line(s)* are repeated, the result being a second Hexagram.

Response - The result of a reading, which consists of one or two Hexagrams.

Resulting texts - If the result of a reading is one Hexagram, these texts are the *Image* and the *Judgment* of the Hexagram. If it consists of two Hexagrams these texts are the *moving Line(s)* in the first Hexagram, both *Images*, and both *Judgments*.

Significant patterns - Given a one- or two-Hexagram result of a reading, these are all the observed *patterns* connecting the *applicable meanings* meaningfully and forming the *theme*.

Significant phrase - For a given reading, the phrase formed with the *applicable meanings* of the resulting Hexagram according to a *significant pattern*. The *most significant phrase* is the *theme of the reading*.

Static Line - A *Line* produced by two heads and a tail (full) or two tails and a head (broken). See *moving line*.

Superior man - A term used in the *I Ching* that refers to the person consulting the *I Ching* or another relevant person or entity.

Surrounding situation - The existing or the final situation.

Table of Hexagram numbers - Table for locating each resulting Hexagram in any *I Ching* book and in this book.

Theme of a reading - The *most significant phrase* formed by the *applicable meanings* of the resulting Hexagrams. Either it contains the answer to the question asked or provides a frame of reference for interpreting the moving *Lines,* the *Images,* and the *Judgments*, and finding if there is an answer.

XII. A Powerful Tool: The Dictionary of the 64 Hexagrams

Why the Dictionary is Necessary

As explained on Chapter III, the set of the 64 Hexagrams viewed as *whole symbols* represents the spectrum of concepts associated with anything that could be *significant* in a reading. It could be a situation, action, event, etc.

Each Hexagram represents a *distinct category* of this spectrum, which is the list of its meanings. The Dictionary presented herein lists the meanings that are essential for decision making, creativity, insight, inspiration, and prediction.

The Dictionary is the link between the *I Ching* and common language because it explains the Hexagrams in terms of everyday words. It is the tool for finding the meanings of a Hexagram that are *applicable* to a reading that results in that Hexagram, so the reading can be as clear and informative as possible.

When using the Dictionary, the role of intuition is clearly defined. For any given reading, this role consists of three steps: a) recognizing the *applicable meanings* of each resulting Hexagram; b) recognizing the most *significant phrase* formed with these meanings, the *theme of that reading*; and c) recognizing the answer—positive or negative—as the *theme*, in the texts of the resulting Hexagrams, or absent, as explained in Chapter III.

How the Dictionary Was Created and Expanded

The Dictionary was compiled: a) for each Hexagram, by taking the concepts from the Wilhelm/Baynes and other *I Ching* books that are compatible and make that Hexagram *unique*, the meanings of that Hexagram; b) by extending the existing Hexagram meanings to closely related meanings and to equivalent meanings in other contexts. For example, "campaign" in Hexagram 7 was extended to "project."

Such extensions were made while preserving the *logical consistency* of the system of Hexagram meanings, according to these two rules:

> 1. Non-conflicting rule: The new meaning does not conflict with any other meaning of that Hexagram.
> 2. Non-overlapping rule: Every meaning can belong to only one Hexagram, since each Hexagram represents a *distinct category* of meanings.

For most Hexagrams, a steady situation is represented by a different Hexagram than the action or change leading to that situation. For instance, "organized" is represented by Hexagram 37 whereas "organizing" is indicated by Hexagram 45; "motivated" is represented by Hexagram 16 and "motivating" by Hexagram 31; "information" is represented by Hexagram 61 and "informing" by Hexagram 27; "control" is represented by Hexagram 34 and "bringing under control" by Hexagram 26, etc.

The more clearly defined the Hexagrams are, the more accurately can the readings be interpreted. For this reason, the words used in the Dictionary have only one principal meaning in English. This makes it easier to find the applicable Hexagram meanings for every reading.

Nouns and verbs in English can sometimes have the same spelling, which could create ambiguity. To differentiate them, verbs appear in the present continuous tense. For example, "group" can be a noun (Hexagram 13, or a verb (Hexagram 45. For this reason, the verb appears as "grouping." If necessary, nouns, verbs and adjectives are indicated by (n), (v), and (adj), respectively, for clarity.

Where appropriate, two related meanings that are represented by the same Hexagram are indicated succinctly like this: "(self) esteem" in Hexagram 16.

To avoid unnecessary duplication, the title of each Hexagram, which is usually one of its meanings, is not repeated in the list of meanings for that Hexagram. For the same reason, if both a verb and the corresponding noun denote the same action, only one of them may be listed. For example, "invasion" implies "invading," Hexagram 57. Likewise, when both a noun and the corresponding adjective denote the same quality, only one of them may be listed. For example, "discouraged" implies "discouragement," Hexagram 47.

In conclusion, the *I Ching* contains a complete set of symbols called Hexagrams. The Dictionary translates each symbol into a list of common words, its respective meanings. When doing a reading, determine which of those meanings are applicable to the reading. The *applicable meanings*, suitably combined, always reveal a meaningful phrase in plain language. This phrase, called the *theme* of the reading, could be the answer or could provide a frame of reference to understand the resulting texts, which may point to the answer. Essentially, this is the approach to interpretation presented in this book.

Keys for Identifying the Hexagrams

Upper 3 lines / Lower 3 lines	☰	☳	☵	☶	☷	☴	☲	☱
☰	1	34	5	26	11	9	14	43
☳	25	51	3	27	24	42	21	17
☵	6	40	29	4	7	59	64	47
☶	33	62	39	52	15	53	56	31
☷	12	16	8	23	2	20	35	45
☴	44	32	48	18	46	57	50	28
☲	13	55	63	22	36	37	30	49
☱	10	54	60	41	19	61	38	58

HEXAGRAM 1

The Creative

(right) action
active
activity
agent
architect
cause (of)
causing
creativity
creator
decider
designing
doer
effecting
effective
entrepreneur
factor
father
generating
great man
industrious
innovating
inventing
maker
making things happen
originator
pioneer
proactive
resourceful
self-made
self-reliance
self-starter

Note: To distinguish between nouns and verbs that have the same spelling in English—like "conduct" as a noun (hexagram 10) and "conduct" as a verb (hexagram 7)—verbs appear in the present continuous tense, as "conducting."

HEXAGRAM 2

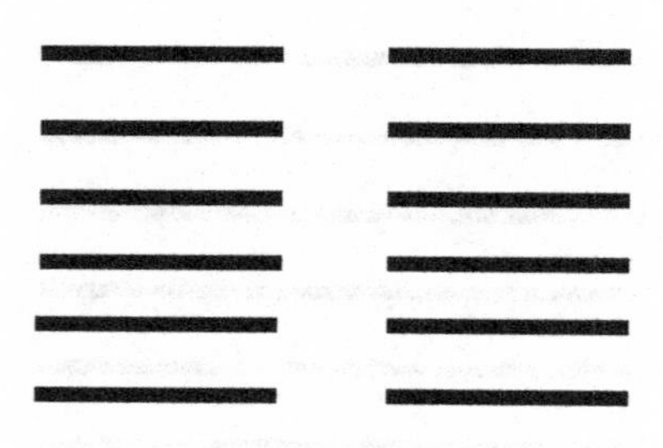

The Receptive

absorbing
accepting
alertness
allowing
antenna
area
assimilating
audience
awareness
being guided
believing
breadth
capacity
consumer
customer
dependent on
detecting
disciple
doorway
earning
earth
embodying
empty
entrance
expanse
experiencing
exposed
feeling
getting
heeding
importing
including
inclusive
inheriting
intuitive
learning
letting in
listening
matter
mother
obtaining
open(ness)
opening
orifice
passive
patient (n)
perceiving
permission
physical
  reality
portal
receiving
receptor
recipient

see next page

HEXAGRAM 2

The Receptive

(Continuation)

seeing
sensing
sensitivity
space
spacious
subject to
subordinated
taking in
taking into account
taking seriously
target
tuned in
undergoing
understanding
vulnerable
welcoming

HEXAGRAM 3

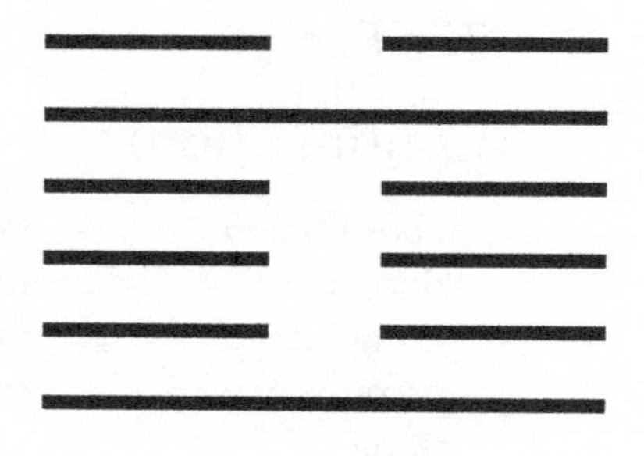

Difficulty at the Beginning

(a) beginning
(giving) birth
bearing fruit
beginner
being born
creating
first (time)
founding
from scratch
inauguration
incipient
initially
just begun
just created
materializing
nascent
new
onset
origin
original
originating
setting out
setting the tone
setting up
starting point
taking shape
threshold
undertaking

HEXAGRAM 4

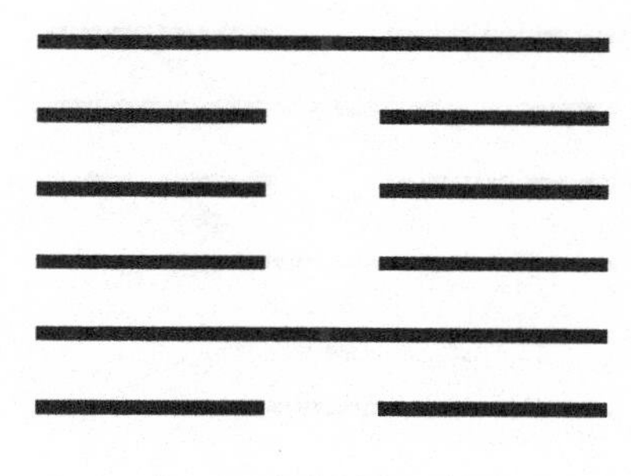

Youthful Folly

absurd
blunder
childish
defect
delusional
doing badly
early stages
error
fantasy
fault
flaw
fool
gaffe
glitch
ignorant
illusion
immaturity
imperfection
impractical
incapable
incorrect
inept
inexperienced
irrational
irresponsible
misconception
misinterpret-
ing
misjudgment
mismanage-
ment
mistake
naïve
nonsense
not right
not right
premature
raw
shortcoming
undeveloped
unfair
unjust
unprepared
unqualified
unrealistic
untamed
vain
wishful
thinking
wrong
young
youth

HEXAGRAM 5

Waiting

anticipating
awaiting
being late
delay
drink
expecting
food
inertia
laziness
leisure
(a) matter of time
meal
patience
pause
postponing
procrastinating
(in a) queue
standby
tolerating

HEXAGRAM 6

Conflict

antagonism
cheating
clash
combat
competition
conflictive
contesting
contradictory
controversial
corrosive
counterpro-
ductive
crime
crisis
deceiving
defiance
delinquent
destructive
dilemma
dishonesty
disputing
distorting
divisive
evil
fallacy
false
fight
fraud
guilty
harmful
illegal
incompatible
inconsistent
infraction
lawsuit
malicious
misdeed
paradox
problematic
quarrelsome
scandal
showdown
toxic
(in) trouble
unacceptable
unconceivable
unhealthy
war (between)

HEXAGRAM 7

The Army

armed
being in charge
campaign
carrying out
conducting
contingent
course of
  action
crusade
diet
directing
direction
doing
driving
endeavor
executive
expedition
fighting for
general (n)
leader(ship)
leading
martial
masses
military
mob
odyssey
performing
plan
police
policing
project
pursuit
quest
regimen
soldier
squadron
strategy
struggle(s)
throng
venture
waging war
warrior
workforce

HEXAGRAM 8

Holding Together [Union]

(in) agreement
(in) alignment
(in) contact
(in) unison
bond
bridge
coherence
cohesive
combination
compact
concentrated
connected
consensus
conserving
continuity
  in space
coordination
director
face to face
head
headquarters
holding
  in common
holistic
in person
inseparable
insuring
integrated
intermediary
intertwined
joint(ly)
keeping
link
loyalty
orchestrated
president
protecting
retaining
robust
ruler
self-contained
self-control
self-sufficient
simultaneous
solid
solidarity
sturdy
synchronicity
synchronized
synergy
synthesis
tight(ly)
together
unanimous
unified
united
whole

HEXAGRAM 9

The Taming Power of the Small

adjusting
affecting
appealing
applicant
barely
beautifying
bid
calibrating
candidate
clue
consulting (v)
control with slight power
critical mass
finesse
fine-tuning
hinting
indirect(ly)
least possible
low-key
manipulating
marginally
mild
minimum
modulating
nuance
polishing
praying
prospect
refining
slight(ly)
slight effect
slow(ly)
small
soft(ly)
soliciting
somewhat
subliminal(ly)
subtle
suitor
swaying
tepid
touching up
tweaking
understatement

HEXAGRAM 10

Treading (Conduct)

behavior
cautious(ly)
conduct (n)
diplomacy
driving (a car)
going
maneuvering
marching
navigating
one step at a time
operating (a machine)
passage
politeness
proceeding
progressing
steering
step by step
stepping into
stepping stone
tactfulness
tactics
taking a step
walking
walking a fine line

HEXAGRAM 11

Peace

adequate
balanced
collaboration
comfortable
compatibility
complement-
ing
cooperation
equilibrium
fairness
fitting in
getting along

give and take
golden mean
(in) good terms
half-way
harmony
health
interdepen-
dence
justice
justified
(perfect) match

mutually
normal(cy)
ok
paired up
peace
reasonable
satisfactory
suitable
middle way
well-being
wellness
win-win

HEXAGRAM 12

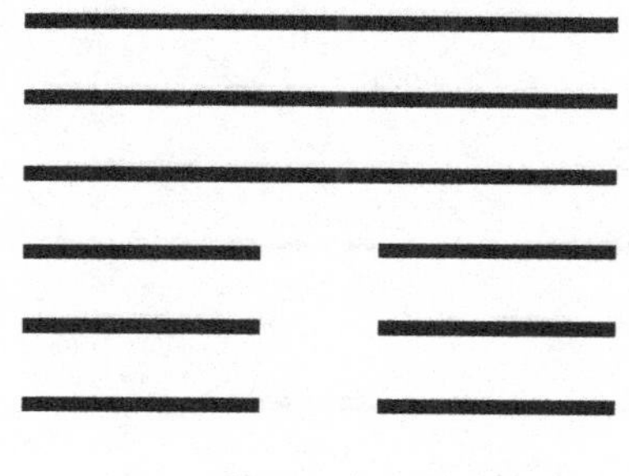

Standstill

absence (of)
alone
aloof
avoidance
away from
blank
dead
detached
disconnection
discontinuity
disjointed
disunion
drought
empty
exempt (from)
free from
gridlock
idle
immune
impasse
impunity
inaction
indifference
ineffective
inert
intact
isolation
lack (of)
loneliness
neutral
nobody
noncommittal
not happening
nothing
numb
out of sync
out of touch
outside (of)
paralysis
seclusion
separated
separation
stagnation
stalemate
stalling
unattached
unemployed
uninvolved
unproductive
unrelated
useless
zero

HEXAGRAM 13

Fellowship with Men

accompanying
accomplice
alliance
ally
amateur
beloved
bunch
category
citizen
clan
class
close friend
club
cluster
coalition
colleague
collectively
committee
(in the)
community
companion
comrade
congregation
constituent
country
dear
equally
equivalent
faction
fan
favorite
fellowship
fond of
going with
(as a) group
helper
like-minded
list
member
nationality
neighbor
parish
peer(s)
political party
profession
race
sibling
siding with
similar
species
team
trade union
type

HEXAGRAM 14

Possession in Great Measure

accredited
affording
asset(s)
capital as
classic
dignity
(the) economy
entitled
equity
established
(the) establishment
financially
goods
having
high
honor
incumbent
installed
inventory
landlord
level
location
money
owner
ownership
owning
placed
platform
(good) position
(right) place
possessing
possession(s)
posture
prestige
privilege
proper
rank
real estate
safe(ty)
score
secure
situation
stable
stage
status
strategic
tall
treasure
upper class
valuable
value
wealthy
well-to-do

HEXAGRAM 15

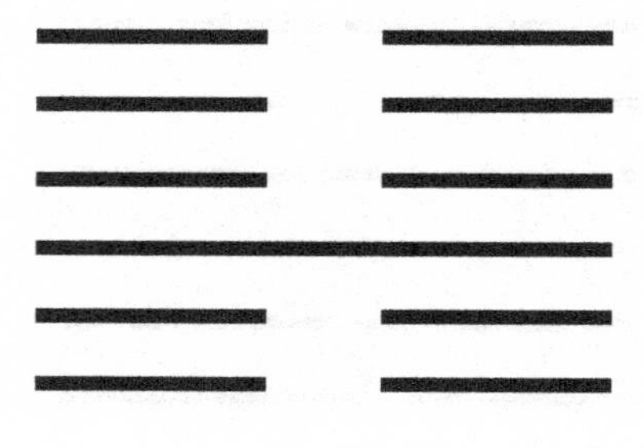

Modesty

abbreviated
accessible
affordable
austerity
auxiliary
(in the) background
common sense
concise
condensed
direct(ly)
doing with less
easy
easygoing

economical
efficiency
effortless
flat
frugality
good enough
horizontal
humility
inexpensive
just enough
lean
low (expectations)
low level

low tech
lowly
low-profile
plain
secondary
shortcut
simplicity
simply
single
slim
straight
unassuming
unsophisticated

HEXAGRAM 16

Enthusiasm

acclaim
aliveness
ambition
appreciation
approving
aspiration
avid
dance
desire
devotion
drama
drive
dynamic
eager
ecstasy
emotion
(self) esteem
exalted
excitement
expectation
faith
(good) feeling
gratitude
happy
heat
honoring
hope
hype
impulse
infatuation
joy
expectation
inspiration
lively
(in) love
militancy
momentum
mood
morale
motivated
motive(s)
muse
(playing) music
optimism
passion
positive
praise
resonance
reverence
rhythm
temperament
thrill
vibration
vocation
wanting
wishing
zeal

HEXAGRAM 17

Following

accordingly
adaptability
addendum
analogy
as expected
building upon
chronological order
consenting
consequently
continuing
resuming
continuity
copying
depending on
deriving(from)
deservedly
effect(s)
ensuing
extrapolating
extending
flexibility
follower
following up
imitating
implication(s)
implying
inevitable
inferring
keeping track
legacy
likewise
next
obeying
prearranged
predictable
projecting
prolonging
pursuing
ramification
responsive
right after
satellite
seeking
(in) sequence
subsequently
subservient
transcribing

HEXAGRAM 18

Work on What Has Been Spoiled [Decay]

altering
correcting
decadence
detoxification
disrepair
doctor
dysfunctional
fixing
healer
illness
ironing out
medical
medicine
mending
modifying
neglected
operation
outdated
overhaul
problem-solving
reactivating
rearranging
reconfiguring
reconstructing
redirecting
reenergizing
reform
reformulating
refreshing
refurbishing
regenerating
rehabilitating
rejuvenating
remedy
renovating
reorganizing
repairing
repositioning
resetting
restructuring
revitalizing
setting right
shift
sluggish
streamlining
therapy
unhealthy
working on or treating

HEXAGRAM 19

Approach

addressing
aiming at
alluding to
approaching
approximating
assigning to
attempting
attracting
becoming
biased
bringing
choosing
closing in
conducive to
convergence
drawing in
electing
estimating
forthcoming
future
going to
gravitating to
guiding
implying
inclined to
likelihood
making a call
manner
method
orienting
pointing at
preferring
preparing for
probable
procedure
propensity
recipe
referring to
selecting
sending to
soon
tendency
tentative
the way (to)
towards
trend
turning to
willingness

HEXAGRAM 20

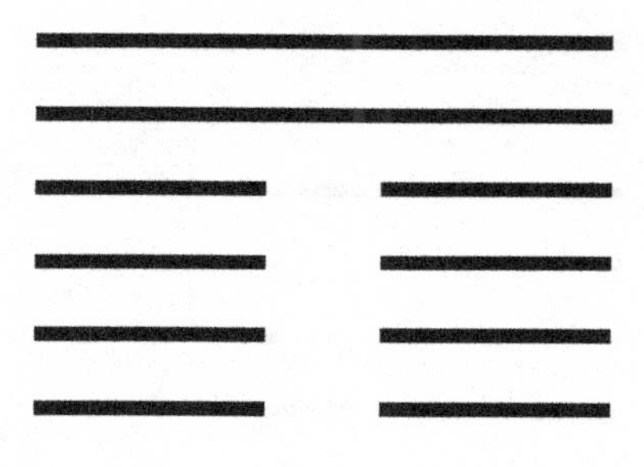

Contemplation (View)

attention
care
careful(ly)
compassion
conceptualiz-
ing
concern
considering
critical
evaluating
examining
focusing on
idol
imagination
inspecting
interviewing
judging

looking for
making sure
making sense
mindfulness
observing
opinion
paradigm
perspective
premeditation
preoccupation
reading (v)
reflection
regarding
respect
reviewing
role model
(being) seen
serious(ness)

speculating
studying
supervision
theory
thinking (of)
thoughtful(ly)
valuing
verifying
view
viewing
viewpoint
vigilance
(a) vision
visualizing
watching
window
witnessing

HEXAGRAM 21

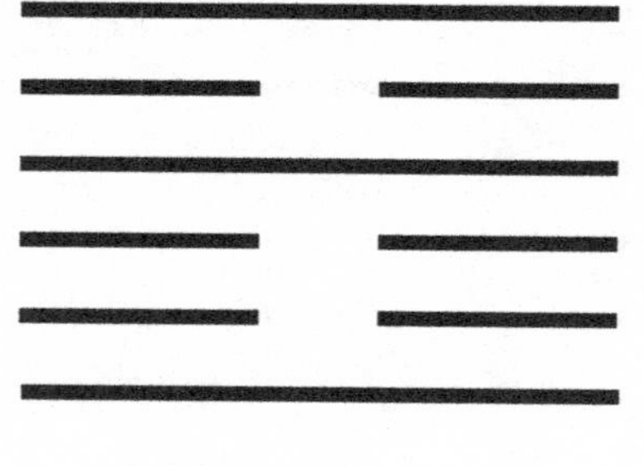

Biting Through

anger
attacking
biting (through obstacles)
brutal
challenge
chewing
combating
complications
cracking down
cruelty
crushing
culprit
cutting
difficulty
drastic
gnawing
harsh
hindrance
hurdle
inconvenience
inflicting
interference
issue (to solve)
penalty
problem
punishing
ruthless
severity
slashing
smashing
uncomfortable
uneasiness
violent
wrath

HEXAGRAM 22

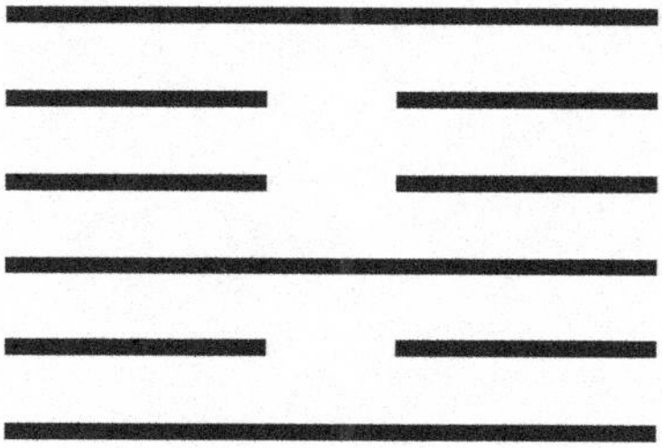

Grace

actor
adornment
apparently
art
beautiful
blueprint
book cover
brand
ceremonial
charisma
charm
cosmetic
courtesy
decorative
elegance
emblem
expression of
external(ly)
fashion
form
formality
good taste
graceful(ly)
illustration
image (of)
looks
map
mask
metaphor
name
nice
non-essential
picture
poise
portraying
presentable
protocol
representing
sample
saving face
seeming(ly)
shape
sign (of)
signal(s)
style
superficial(ly)
(on the) surface
symbol (of)
symptom
theatre
veneer

HEXAGRAM 23

Splitting Apart

bankruptcy
breach
breaking (up)
breaking a rule
 or habit
breaking loose
broken
cancelling
caving in
collapsing
contradicting
crack
crumbling
cutting up
declining
denying
destruction

detaching
disassociating
disconnecting
disengaging
dismantling
disowning
dissecting
divorce
downfall
failure
fission
fracture(d)
interrupting
intoxication
parting (ways)
peeling off

refusing
refuting
rejecting
repudiating
rescinding
revoking
rupture
sabotaging
separating
severing
splitting
stripping
tearing off
ripping
undercutting
undermining
unraveling

HEXAGRAM 24

Return (The Turning Point)

about-face
again
alternating
back and forth
back on track
backlash
bouncing
change of mind
coming back
counteracting
cyclic
embryonic
giving back
imminent
impending
in and out
in return
insisting
on the verge
periodically
reaction
reciprocating
reconsidering
recovery
recurring
recursive
recycling
reincarnation
reinstating
remorse
renaissance
renewal
repeating
repenting
reply
response
restitution
restoration
resurgence
retaliation
retribution
retro(active)
reversing
reverting to
revisiting
rewinding
seed
taking back
tipping point
turnaround
turning back
undoing
wavering

HEXAGRAM 25

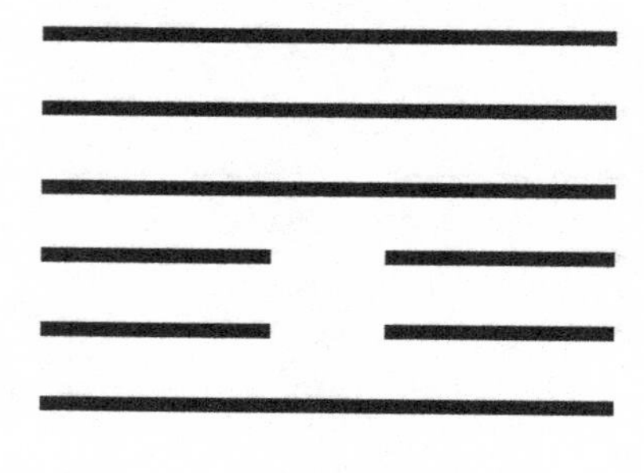

Innocence [The Unexpected]

(by) accident
amazing
animal
autonomy
blameless
by chance
casually
contingency
faultless
free to
having no expectations
having no idea
improvised
in the moment
incidentally
independent
innately
instinctive(ly)
involuntarily
let it be
magical
miracle
not according to
not knowing
on impulse
out of the blue
(at) random
serendipity
spontaneous
surprise
thoughtless
unaware (of)
unconscious
uncontrolled
undeserved
unexpected
unexplained
unintended
unplanned
unprecedented
unpredictable
unprovoked
unwarranted
unwitting(ly)
virgin
wild
with no pre-conceived notions
without ulterior motives
without one's intervention

HEXAGRAM 26

The Taming Power of the Great

abstaining
accumulating
bringing
  under control
collecting
  oneself
containment
defense against
detaining
deterring
disciplining
domesticating
harnessing
holding one's
  ground
holding
  judgment
holding back
holding in
  check
inhibiting
pent up
prevention
refraining from
reining in
repressing
resisting
restraining
reticent
saving money
  time or
  energy
sparing (v)
storing
subduing
subjugating
taming
withholding
withstanding

HEXAGRAM 27

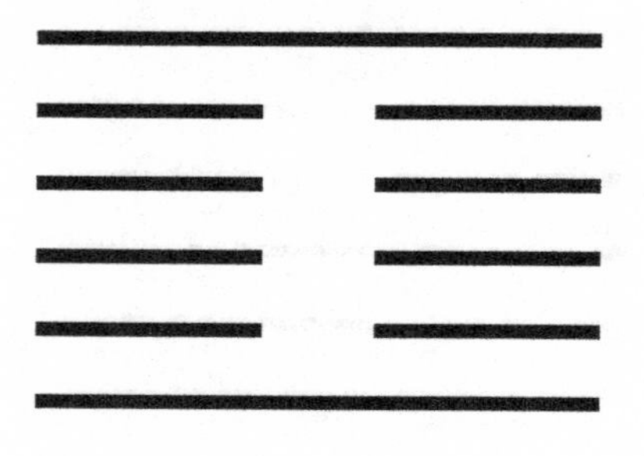

The Corners of the Mouth
(Providing Nourishment)

artery
budgeting
caretaker
commenting
communi-
cating
concession
contributing
counseling
cultivating
describing
drinking
eating
educating
explaining
advising
feeding
financing
food chain
fueling
funding
giving
income
informing
instructing
justifying
language
lifeline
maintenance
message
mouth
nourishing
nursing
offering
payment
providing
recommending
reporting
serving
supplying
taking care of
telling
upkeep
vocabulary
voicing
word(s)

HEXAGRAM 28

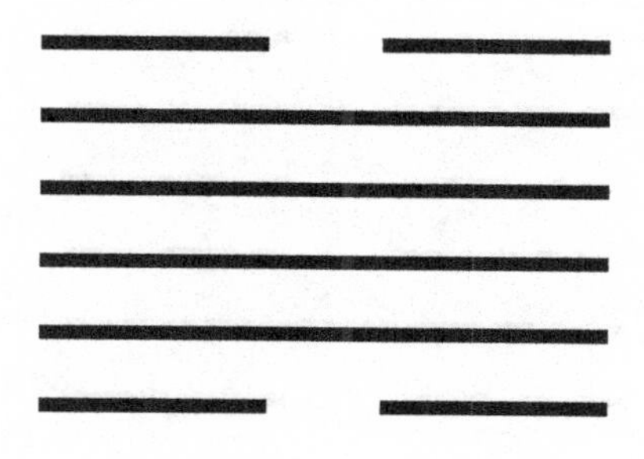

Preponderance of the Great

abuse
arbitrary
awkward
crisis
disproportion
egregious
flagrant
fragile
heavy
inadequate
inappropriate
indefensible
inefficient
insecure
intolerable
need
old
one-sided
out of place
overburdened
overwhelmed
precarious
requiring intervention
sagging
shaky
shame
unbalanced
unbearable
unequal (to)
uninsured
unjustified
unnecessary
unsafe
unstable
unsuitable
unsupported
unsustainable
untenable
wasteful
weak

HEXAGRAM 29

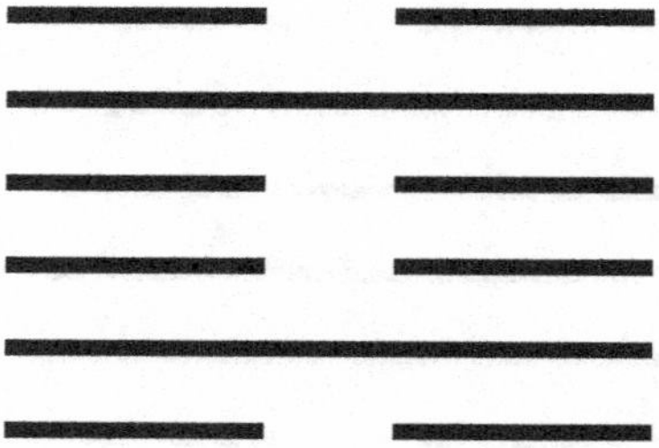

The Abysmal (Water)

abysmal
abyss
blood
(hitting) bottom
catastrophe
(fraught with) danger
dangerous
debt
depths
disaster
endangering
flood
fluid
immeasurable
immensity
infinite
jeopardizing
low point
mystery
ocean
ominous
pit
pitfall
(at) risk
scary or delicate situation
subconscious
submerged
(the) unknown
threat
under
unfathomable
unfortunate
valley
water

HEXAGRAM 30

The Clinging, Fire

ablaze
adhering (to)
bondage
brilliance
burning
caught
certainty
certifying
clarity
(making) clear
clinging (to)
enlightening
entanglement
evident
explicit(ly)
eyes
fame
glow
hostage
illuminating
knowing
light
logical
lucid
luminous
luster
net
official(ly)
prison
proof
proving
realistic
reassuring
remembering
shining
showing
siege
star
sticking with
sticky
sun
transparent
trap
trapped
unequivocal
visible

HEXAGRAM 31

Influencing (Wooing)

alluring
applying for
asking
attraction
calling forth
catalyst
commanding
courtship
curiosity
demanding
eliciting
encouraging
enticing
evoking
exciting (v)
fascination
flirting
general (adj.)
hypnosis
incentive
inciting
inducing
inquiring
instigating
interested
inviting
invoking
magnet(ism)
motivating
persuading
prompting
provoking
question(ing)
requesting
seducing
(casting a) spell
spurring
stimulating
summons
tempting
universal
urging

HEXAGRAM 32

Duration

all the time
always
carrying on
character
consistently
constantly
continually
continuity in time
diehard
durability
enduring
era
existing
habitual
incessantly
inflexible
irreversible
keeping up
lasting
leftover
lifetime
(a) long time
(in the) long run
long-term
longevity
obstinate
ongoing
perseverance
persistence
relentless
remaining
residual
resilience
rigid
sameness
season
self-sustaining
so far
stamina
staying
staying alive
staying the course
steadfast
steady
surviving
sustainability
tenacity
tireless
unswerving

HEXAGRAM 33

Retreat

abandoning
averting
avoiding
backwards
leaving
behind
defection
departing
deserting
disappearing
discarding
(creating)
distance
dodging
drawing from
eliminating

elusive
emanating
backing off
evading
evasiveness
extracting
farewell
flowing from
getting (more)
detached
giving in
going away
going some-
where else
gone
hiding

leaking
quitting
receding
recession
relenting
removing
retirement
retrenching
setting aside
shrinking
stealing (from)
taking away
stepping back
suppressing
turning away
from

HEXAGRAM 34

The Power of the Great

authority
being able
capability
clout
coercion
compelling
(in) control
dominance
driving force
energy
engine
force

(being) forced
imposing
jurisdiction
leverage
loud
mastery
motor
muscle
(having an) option
overbearing

overpowering
overriding
(having a) permit
(making) possible
preponderance
prerogative
strength
superpower
upper hand
willpower

HEXAGRAM 35

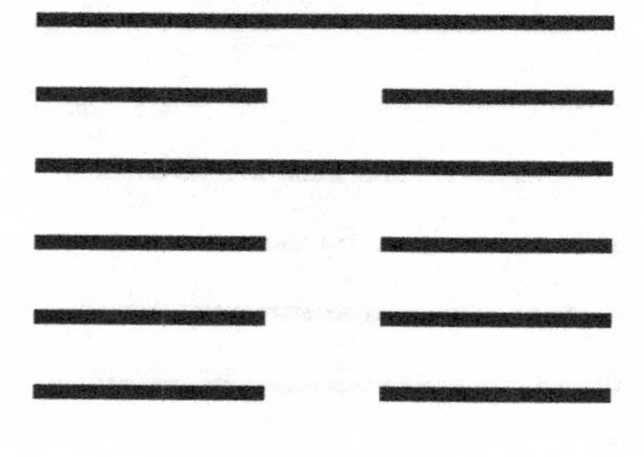

Progress

advancing
amplifying
better (than)
blooming
doing better
expanding
(fast) forward
forwarding
further ahead
growth
improvement
leap
moving on
moving or placing ahead
multiplying
onward
progressive
promoting
prospering
superior (to)
thriving
widening

HEXAGRAM 36

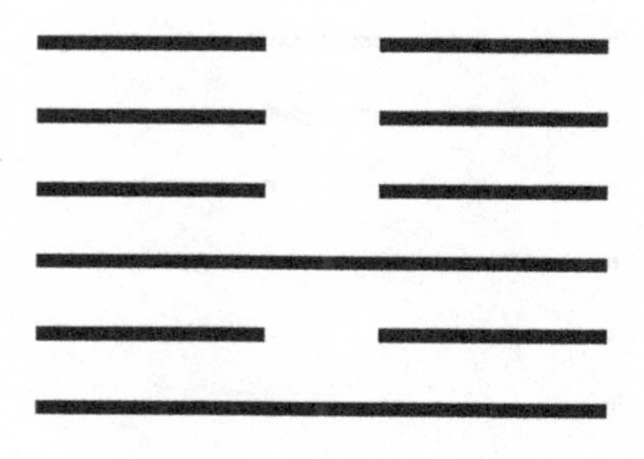

Darkening of the Light

ambiguous
anonymous
behind (the scenes)
behind one's back
camouflage
clandestine
cloudy
concealing
confusing
confusion
corruption
covering up
darkening
defacing
dirty
discrediting
disguising
(in) doubt
furtive
harm
hurting
indirect
injury
invisible
latent
not obvious
obscuring
offending
pollution
pretending
reserve
secretive
sneaky
soiled
tainted
telling a lie
uncertainty
unclear
undeclared
under the table
undercover
unspoken
unsure
vague
veiled
wound

HEXAGRAM 37

The Family

applicable
between
complement
configuration
conjugal
connection
context
correlation
corresponding
couple
domain
domestic
environment
framework
having to do with
hierarchy
(at) home
household
in relation to
institution
interaction
interface
interplay
network
organization
organized
participating
(in) proportion
range
rapport
relatedness
relationship
relative to
relative(s)
relevant
role
social life
society
spouse
structure
system
ties

HEXAGRAM 38

Opposition

across from
adversary
(being or going) against
alienation
alternative
(an)other
anti-
classifying
comparing
contrasting
differentiating
denying
despite
dichotomy
difference
disagreement
disapproval
discrepancy
discriminating
disobedience
dislike
dissatisfaction
distinct
diversity
don't
either-or
(someone) else
estrangement
excluding
individualism
mistrust
negativity
not (being)
opposed
opposite (of)
polarization
reluctance
resentment
reverse
skepticism
sorting out
subdividing
tension
the other(side)
unpopular
unsociable
unwanted
unwilling
upside down

HEXAGRAM 39

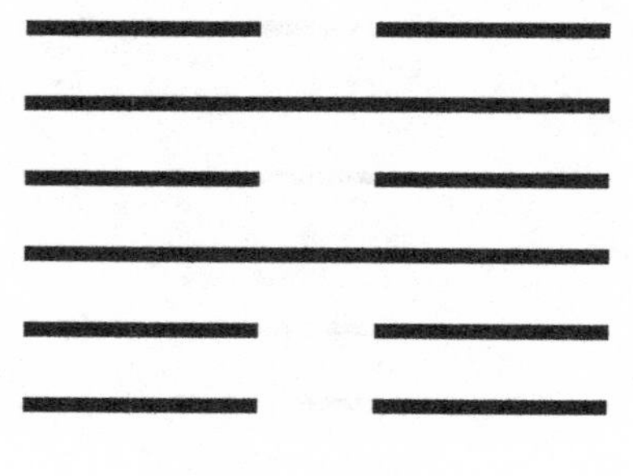

Obstruction

air-tight
barrier
blind
blockade
blocking
clogged up
closed (off)
close-minded
covering
deaf
difficult
eclipsing
embargo
impassable
impeded
impeding
impenetrable
impossible
inaccessible
insensitive
insulation
insurmounta-
ble
intercepting
keeping from
not allowing
not seeing
obstacle
obstructing
off-limits
precluding
proscription
protection
against
quarantine
roadblock
sealed
shield
shut (off)
unable
unattainable
unavailable
undoable
unreachable
veil
wall

HEXAGRAM 40

Deliverance

acquitting
as soon as possible
bailout
cleansing
clearing (up)
delivering
disclosing
dispatching
easing
ejecting
emptying
escape
evacuation
exhaling
exit
exorcising
exporting
exposing
extricating
getting out
issuing
letting go
letting out
liberation
opening up
output
producing
purging
purifying
releasing
relieving
relinquishing
rescue
revealing
salvation
selling
sending out
setting free
shooting
throwing out
tossing
unblocking
uncovering
unleashing
unlocking
urgency
venting

HEXAGRAM 41

Decrease

abbreviating
abridging
alleviating
attenuating
being more specific or specialized
compressing
cooling off
cost
damaging
decreasing
defeat
degrading
demeaning
depriving
derogatory
descending
deteriorating
disadvantage
disparaging
down(ward)
downgrading
downplaying
economizing expenses
facilitating
falling
fee
giving up
humiliation
less
lessening
loss(es)
lower(ing)
marginalizing
minimizing
missing an opportunity
narrowing down
plunge
reducing (to)
relegating
sacrifice
shrinking
simplifying
sinking
slowing down
surrendering
tax
trimming
weakening
worsening

HEXAGRAM 42

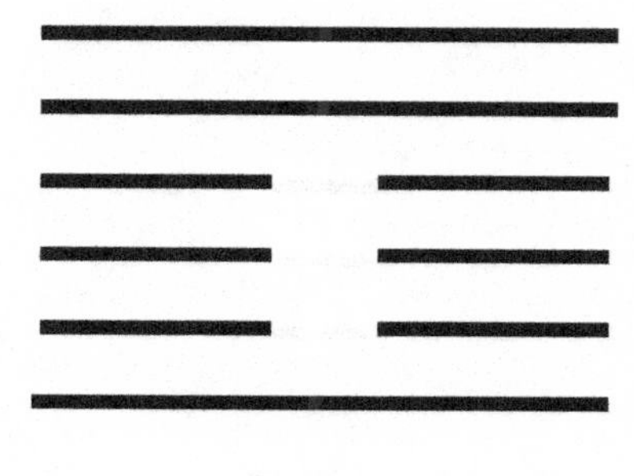

Increase

adding to
additionally
advantage
altruism
assisting
augmenting
authorizing
awarding
backing up
benefit(ting)
benevolence
bequeathing
blessing
bonus
charity
comforting
donation
empowering
enabling
endorsing
enhancing
enriching
favor
favorable
favoring
for free
forgiving
fortifying
(good) fortune
gain
generosity
gift
giving energy
goodwill
granting
handing down
helping
intensifying
invigorating
kindness
leniency
loving
luck
more
pardoning
philanthropy
preferable
propitious
reinforcing
selfless
silver lining
sponsoring
supplementing
thanks to
upgrading
warranty

HEXAGRAM 43

Break-through (Resoluteness)

advertising
affirming
announcing
asserting
assertiveness
boldness
book
bravery
breaking the impasse
claim
courage
daring to
decision
decisive
declaration
decree
denouncing
determination
dislodging
document
evicting
expelling
expressing
finest hour
formulating
landslide
making known
news
nominating
ousting
outspoken
pledge
preaching
proclaiming
promulgating
pronouncing
publicizing
publishing
pushing out
(re)solution
resolve
sanctioning
saying
speaking up
statement
text
triumph
verdict
victory
warning

HEXAGRAM 44

Coming to Meet

accommodating to
approach
arriving
attaining
attunement
available
catching up
conforming to
connecting
coping with
dating
dealing with
engaging (v)
facing
finding
getting to meet
in-person
harmonizing
installing
interceding
intersecting
landing
making contact
massage
matching
mediating
networking
placing
plugging
presence
reaching (a compromise)
running into
satisfying requirements
showing up
socializing
synchronizing
tailoring to
there is
touching

HEXAGRAM 45

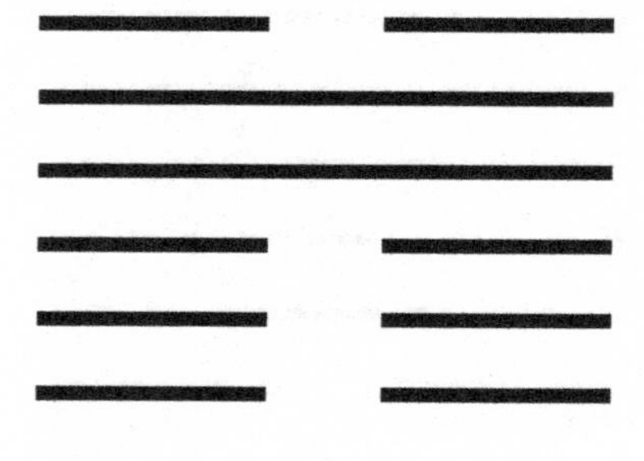

Gathering Together (Massing)

acquiring
adopting
appropriating
arranging
articulating
assembling
attaching (to)
becoming part
blending
bonding
capturing
combining
coming to an
 agreement
compiling
completing
composing
compounding
concentrating
configuring
consolidating
constructing
crystallizing
documenting
embracing
firming up
gathering
getting
 involved
harmonizing
harnessing
incorporating
amassing
integrating
joining
merging
mixing
organizing
picking up
possessiveness
putting
 together
reaping
recollecting
reconciling
recruiting
taking
 control
 charge
tightening up
totaling
uniting
writing a book

HEXAGRAM 46

Pushing Upward

accentuating
appointing
ascending
boosting
building up
doing one's best
dramatizing
elevating
emphasizing
establishing
exaggerating
exalting
exercise
exertion
forceful
forcing
getting up
glorifying
labor
launching
lifting
moving up
optimizing
piling (up)
practice
pressing
propelling
pulling up
pumping
pushing (the limits)
putting energy into
self-improvement
stressing
upholding
uplifting
uploading
upwards
validating
vigorously
work as effort
workout

HEXAGRAM 47

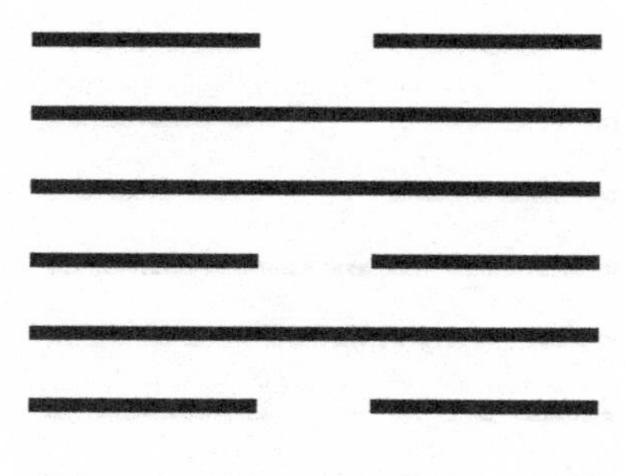

Oppression (Exhaustion)

accusing
aging
annoying
arduous
attrition
bothering
burned out
complaining
criticizing
death
depleting
deteriorating
disappointment
discomfort
discouraged
draining
drowning
drying up
dwindling
dying out
expiring
extinction
failing
fatigue
friction
frustration
getting bored
grieving
grueling
harassment
(having a) hard time
hardship
irritating
languishing
letting down
misery
old
pain
plight
poverty
predicament
running out of
 energy
 money
 patience
 interest
sad
squeezing
starving
straining
torment
tribulation
upsetting
using up
wearing out
withering

HEXAGRAM 48

The Well

ancestor
ancestral
archives
basic as
(the) Collec-
tive Uncon-
scious (Jung)
 fundamental
basis
dependable
employing
essential
exploiting
foundation
fountain
here & now
indispensable
infrastructure
livelihood
memory
mine
necessary
organic
practical
prerequisite
record(s)
recourse
reliable
reservoir
resorting to
resource
root
school
source (of)
supply
support
sustaining
underlying
underneath
useful
using
utilizing

HEXAGRAM 49

Revolution (Molting)

(choosing an) alternative
change
exchange
in place of
instead of
inverting
making a difference
mutating
overturning
permutation
replacing
revolutionary
revolutionizing
shifting
substitution
switch
trading
transposing

HEXAGRAM 50

The Caldron

accomplish-
ment
achievement
artifact
artificial
brewing
by means of
chemistry
clever
computer
contrived
converting
cooking
crafting
device
digesting
elaborating
engineering
equipment
equipped
functional
functioning
gadget
hi-tech
industry
installation(s)
instrument
kitchen
laboratory
machine
making
man-made
manufacturing
masterpiece
means
(to an end)
mechanism
organ (anat.)
processing
processor
result(s)
shop
skill
technical
technology
tool
transformation
transforming
transformative
translating
transmuting
trick
vessel
weapon

HEXAGRAM 51

The Arousing (Shock, Thunder)

activating
agitation
alarm
alerting
anxiety
arising
awakening
disruption
disturbance
jolt
earliest
earthquake
emerging
enacting
epiphany
eruption
expediting
explosion
fear
frightening
happening
hectic
hurrying
igniting
immediately
impact(ful)
initiating
initiative
jumping
leading edge
making or be-
coming aware
noise
panic
recognizing
riot
shaking up
shocking
skyrocketing
starting
stirring up.
sudden(ly)
surge
taking action
switching on
trembling
upheaval
uprising
vanguard
wake-up call

HEXAGRAM 52

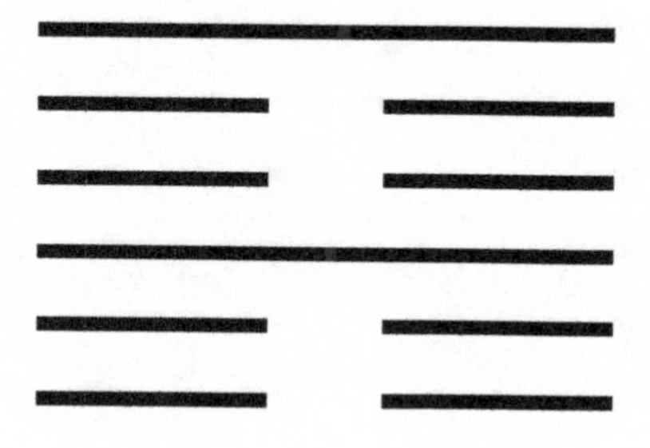

Keeping Still   Mountain

(putting on
the) brakes
calm
calming down
cessation
deactivating
fixed
freezing (v)
halting
immobilizing
meditation
mountain
not moving
putting a stop
quiet
quieting
resting
settling down
silence
silencing
stationary
staying
stilling
stillness
stopping
switching off
tranquility
unchangeable
undisturbed
unmovable
veto

HEXAGRAM 53

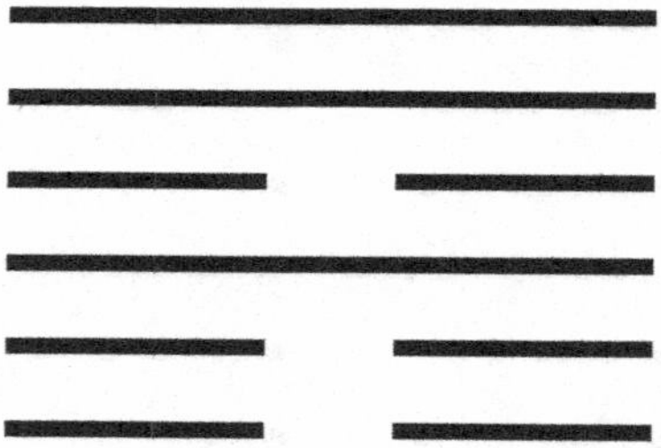

Development (Gradual Progress)

career
developing
escalating
evolution
evolving

gradually
growing
in progress
in the course of time
in the making

inflating
maturing
process
progression
transition

HEXAGRAM 54

The Marrying Maiden

busy (with)
commitment
contract
deal
duty
employed
engaged
implicated
invested in
involvement
lady
marriage
obligation
occupation as job or business
occupied with
pact
settlement

HEXAGRAM 55

Abundance

abundant
advanced
amount
best (possible)
bloated
climax
clutter
complex
complicated
congested
culmination
density
enough
excellent
excessive
frequent
glory
great(ly)
highly
intricate
large(-scale)
magnitude
mainstream
many
(opportunities
or occasions)
mature
maximum
(the) most
much
multi-
multidiscipli-
nary
multiple
number (of)
percentage
plenty
prevalent
probable
profusion
pronounced
prosperity
quantity
rampant
remarkable
richness
ripe
several
size
splendor
superb
thickness
very
waste(ful)

HEXAGRAM 56

The Wanderer

adventure
affair
brief(ly)
browsing
circulating
current(ly)
cursory
errand
explorer
exploring
flash
fleeting
for the time being
foreign
gambling
glance
going around

guest
hasty
itinerant
momentary
newcomer
nomadic
occasion
opportunity
outsider
passenger
passer-by
preliminary
quick(ly)
ride
roaming
short trip
short-lived

short-term
stranger
summarily
surveying
taking a risk
temporary
timely
tour
tourist
transferring
transitory
transmitting
transporting
traveling
trying out
venturing
visit(or)
wandering

HEXAGRAM 57

The Gentle (The Penetrating, Wind)

access(ing)
analyzing
deepening
discovering
divination
entering
experimenting
introducing
far-reaching
figuring out
foreseeing
getting into
getting the point across
getting to know
going into
going through
immigrating
infiltrating
infusing
inhaling
injecting
inoculation
input
inquisitive
inserting
inspiring
instilling
internalizing
interpreting
intervention
introspection
invasion
investigating
investing (in)
key
pervading
piercing
planting
printing
probing
putting into
recording
scoring
searching through
seeing beyond
sharp
taking root
wind
wood

HEXAGRAM 58

The Joyous, Lake

amusing
bathing
being liked
body of water
conference
conversation
debate
deliberation
delight
dialogue
discussion
enjoying
entertaining
fulfillment
fun
gratifying
indulging in
liking
liquid
lubricating
metal
negotiating
pleasing
pleasure
popularity
satisfaction
savoring
soaking
solace
talking with
tasting

HEXAGRAM 59

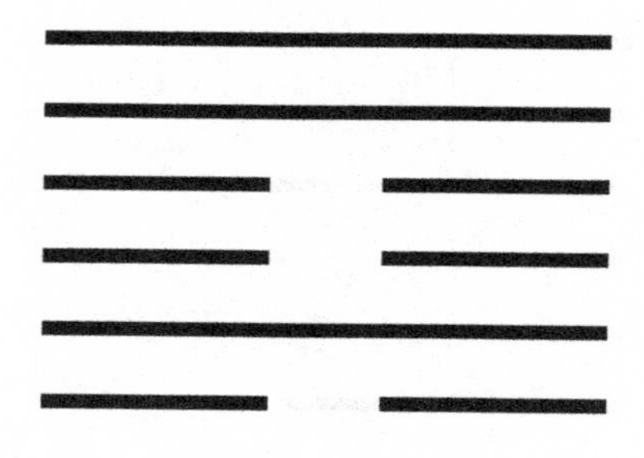

Dispersion (Dissolution)

annihilation
(far) apart
blurring
broadcasting
chaos
crossing the great water
decentralizing
deflecting
defusing
delegating
deploying
derailing
deviation
diffusion
digression
diluting
disarray
dispelling
dispersing
disregarding
dissemination
dissipating
dissolving
distance
distraction
distributing
diverging
diversifying
diversion
divulging
entropy
extinguishing
factionalism
forgetting
generalizing
getting lost
journey
lightening up
loosening up
marketing
melting
neglecting
outreach
popularizing
radiation
scattering
sharing
spreading
vaporization
widespread
wiping out

HEXAGRAM 60

Limitation

(setting) boundaries
budgeting
calculating
circumstances
compart- mentalizing
conditionally
conditioned
confining (one- self or others)
constraint
counting
curbing
deadline
(well) defined
defining
(de)limiting
discipline
drawing the line
edge
exclusively
filter
law(ful)
limit
local(ized)
individually
locating
measuring
mediocre
modularized
morality
narrow- minded
norm(s)
only
ordinary
parameters
partially
policy
prudence
quality control
regulating
requirements
restricting
rule(s)
selective
specializing in
specific
stipulation
strict
up to a point

HEXAGRAM 61

Inner Truth

accuracy
attribute
authentic
being (v)
belief
belonging
centered
central
conscience
content(s)
conviction(s)
core
credibility
deep
essence
exactly
gist (of)
honest(ly)
idea
ideal
identity
implicit
individuality
indwelling
information
ingrained
inhabitant
inherent
innate
inner
inside
insight
intending
intention
intimate
intrinsic
knowledge
legitimate
meaning(ful)
mission as goal
potential(ly)
precisely
principle(s)
purpose
quality
secret
sincerity
soul (of)
truth
truthful
unique(ness)
unrevealed
valid
virtue
wisdom

HEXAGRAM 62

Preponderance of the Small

(going) beyond
bypassing
detail-oriented
exceeding
exception
exceptional
extra
extraordinary
extreme(ly)
fussy
going overboard
going the extra mile
going too far
meticulous
outgrowing
outlier
outperforming
outsmarting
overcoming
overdoing
overflowing
overkill
overshooting
painstaking
passing (n)
passing (by)
peak experience
perfectionism
prevailing
rising over
skipping
standing out
surmounting
surpassing
transcending
unusual

HEXAGRAM 63

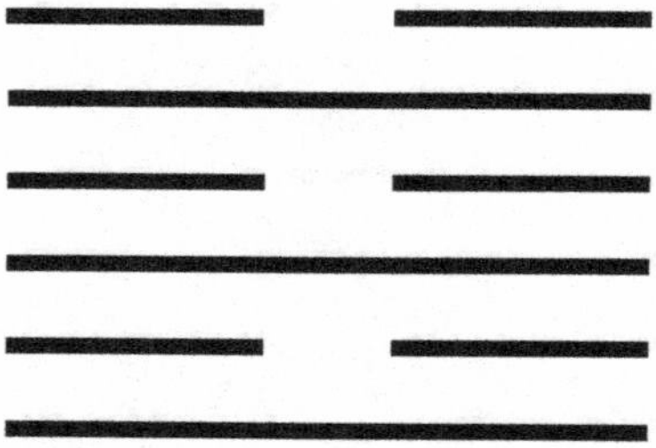

After Completion

absolute(ly)
achieving
all
coming to an end
completely
completion
comprehensive
conclusion
conclusive
consummation
definitive
destination
done
(in the) end
eventually
every
everyone
exhaustive
final
final(ly)
finale
finished
full cycle
full(y)
full-fledged
happened
integrity
last (adj.)
perfection
pure(ly)
ready
success
supreme
thorough
totality

HEXAGRAM 64

Before Completion

almost
imperfect
incomplete
inconclusive
insufficient
less than
nearly
needing completion
not completely
not enough
not final
not quite
not ready
not yet
pending
unfinished
unresolved
unsuccessful
unsatisfactory
unfulfilled

If you have any questions, want to inquire about our classes or consulting services, or would like to invite the author to speak at an event you are hosting please send an e-mail to:
Idecide123@yahoo.com

To see more readings, to share your thoughts about this book, or to purchase this book, please visit our website/blog:
TheLogicOfChance.com

Made in the USA
Middletown, DE
04 February 2024

48465043R00113